ALFRED'S

PIANO 101

148231

AN EXCITING GROUP COURSE FOR ADULTS
WHO WANT TO PLAY PIANO FOR FUN!

BOOK 2

E. L. LANCASTER / KENON D. RENFROW

D1558121

Foreword

Piano 101, Book 2, is a group course designed for adults who have successfully completed *Piano 101, Book 1,* or have previously attained a similar level of proficiency. Its easy-to-use format also is effective in private lessons. Specifically, it can be used for college piano classes of non-music majors, continuing education classes and music dealer in-store programs.

Piano 101 is easy to use. It contains 15 units. In college classes for non-music majors, each unit is designed to be covered in one week, thus filling an entire semester of study. However, teachers who are using the book in college classes or other situations should move at a pace appropriate for each individual class. The title page of each unit contains the objectives for the unit, a space to record assignments and a section called *"Did You Know?"* This section briefly discusses elements of music history or music theory of general interest to piano students. It can serve as a spring board for further class discussion. Major headings (including all new concepts) are identified by a check mark (✓). Measures are numbered in all examples to promote ease of use in the classroom.

The reading approach is eclectic, combining the best elements of intervallic and multi-key reading. Reading exercises are designed to promote movement over the entire keyboard while maintaining the advantages of playing in familiar positions. Reading examples are a mixture of familiar music and newly composed pieces.

Suggestions for counting are given but the approach used is left to the discretion of the teacher. Rhythms and note values are introduced systematically and specially designed rhythm reading exercises promote rhythmic security.

The student begins to play music immediately. Repertoire has been carefully chosen to appeal to adults who are playing the piano for fun and includes tasteful arrangements of familiar music. A section of supplementary repertoire begins on page 119 for those students who need additional music or for teachers who like a wider choice of music for students. The supplementary repertoire was chosen to represent a variety of levels and can be used throughout the book.

Each unit contains a balance of new information with materials that reinforce concepts presented in previous units. Written review worksheets appear periodically throughout the text.

Theory, technique, sight-reading, repertoire, harmonization from lead sheets, ear training and ensemble activities are taught thoroughly and consistently throughout the text. The emphasis on ear training and harmonizing melodies from lead sheets will be helpful to those students who are interested in playing by ear. Teacher's examples for all ear training examples are contained in Appendix A (page 145).

Technique is developed in a systematic way throughout the entire book. Repertoire, lead sheet melodies, technical exercises and sight-reading examples are carefully fingered to aid the student in developing good technique.

This book is fully supported by Compact Discs (CD) and General MIDI (GM) disks. Each example in the text that contains an accompaniment is identified by an icon that shows the disk number and TRACK number for the example: 🔊 **1-1(33)**. The first number after the icon denotes the CD/GM disk number. The second number is the TRACK number on the CD and the Type 0 MIDI file on the GM disk. The third number (in parentheses) is the TRACK number of the Type 1 MIDI file on the GM disk. (See MIDI disk documentation for more information on MIDI file types.) Accompaniments range from simple drum patterns to full orchestrations. These accompaniments add musical interest and motivate students to complete assignments both in the classroom and in the practice room.

A Teacher's Handbook for the text serves as an aid in curriculum development and daily lesson planning. The Handbook contains suggested daily lesson plans, suggested assignments following each lesson plan, teaching tips for each unit, suggested examinations for the semester and answer keys for the written exercises and review worksheets. It also suggests ways to successfully integrate keyboard and computer technology into the curriculum.

Upon completion of this book, students will have a strong grasp of keyboard skills, piano repertoire and musical styles, to allow them to play for fun and pursue further study.

Table of Contents

PIANO 101, BOOK 2

Major and Minor Five-Finger Patterns and Triads (Review)

Objectives

Upon completion of this unit the student will be able to:

1. Play major and minor five-finger patterns and triads beginning on any white key.
2. Perform duet repertoire with a partner.
3. Perform solo repertoire that uses five-finger patterns and chords.
4. Sight-read music that uses five-finger patterns.
5. Tap two-part rhythm patterns

Assignments

Week of _____

Write your assignments for the week in the space below.

_____

_____

_____

_____

_____

_____

_____

_____

_____

_____

_____

_____

Did You Know?

Famous Pianists

The history of piano playing began with Wolfgang Amadeus Mozart and Muzio Clementi in the Classical period. Continuing into the Romantic period, Franz Liszt created hysteria with his piano recitals throughout Europe. Stories abound of ladies fainting when Liszt played the piano; others threw their jewels on the stage rather than flowers. While Liszt was probably the first to give solo recitals without the aid of other musicians, it was Clara Schumann who first played recitals from memory. Pianists such as Sergei Rachmaninoff, Artur Rubinstein and Vladimir Horowitz developed huge followings in the United States during the 20th century. It was a young Texan, Van Cliburn, who captured the hearts of the American public in 1958 when he won the Moscow International Tchaikovsky Competition. Today piano competitions abound throughout the world and numerous pianists enter them with hopes of sparking an international concert career.

Wolfgang Amadeus Mozart

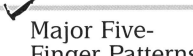

Major Five-Finger Patterns

A major five-finger pattern is a series of five notes having the pattern: *whole step, whole step, half step, whole step.*

LH five-finger patterns are fingered 5 4 3 2 1.
RH five-finger patterns are fingered 1 2 3 4 5.

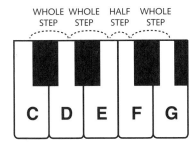

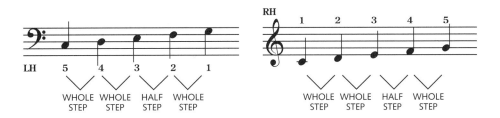

Minor Five-Finger Patterns

A minor five-finger pattern is a series of five notes having the pattern: *whole step, half step, whole step, whole step.*

LH five-finger patterns are fingered 5 4 3 2 1.
RH five-finger patterns are fingered 1 2 3 4 5.

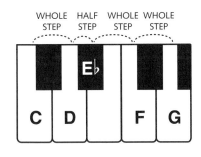

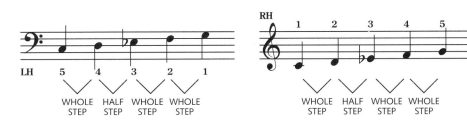

Triads (Chords)

A **triad** is a three-note chord. The three notes of a triad are the root (1), the third (3), and the fifth (5). The **root** is the note from which the triad gets its name. The root of a C triad is C. Triads in root position (with the root at the bottom) always look like this:

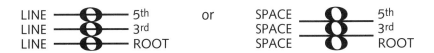

LH chords are fingered 5 3 1. RH chords are fingered 1 3 5.

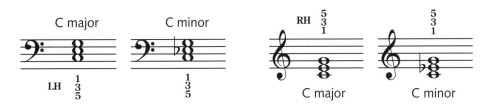

Major five-finger patterns and chords become minor when the
middle note is lowered a half step.

Major Five-Finger Pattern and Chord:

Minor Five-Finger Pattern and Chord:

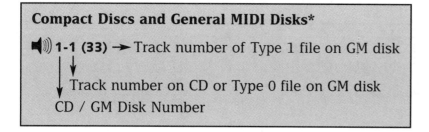

Compact Discs and General MIDI Disks*

🔊 **1-1 (33)** ➤ Track number of Type 1 file on GM disk

Track number on CD or Type 0 file on GM disk

CD / GM Disk Number

Play the following exercise that uses major and minor five-finger
patterns and chords.

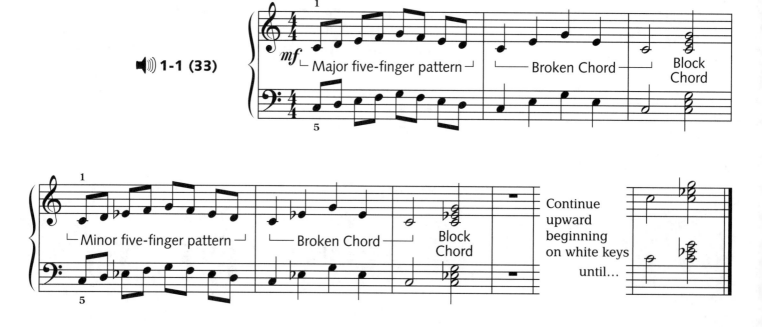

🔊 **1-1 (33)**

READING

Play the following example counting aloud.

🔊 1-2 (34)

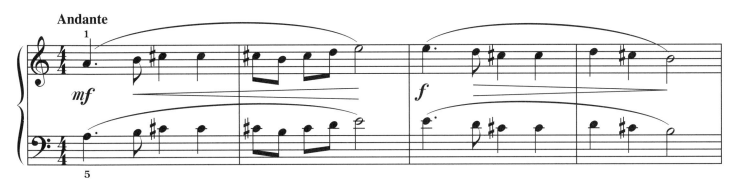

RHYTHM READING

Tap the following rhythm patterns using RH for notes with stems going up and LH for notes with stems going down. Tap hands separately first, and then hands together, always counting aloud.

🔊 1-3 (35)

1.

🔊 1-4 (36)

2.

🔊 1-5 (37)

3.

🔊 1-6 (38)

4.

Polka

from *Ingenuità*

Ernesto Becucci (1845–1905)
Op. 308, No. 2

1-7 (39)

Allegro

DUET: PRIMO

Student

Polka

from *Ingenuità*

Ernesto Becucci (1845–1905)
Op. 308, No. 2

1-7 (39)

Allegro

(Both hands two octaves higher than written throughout)

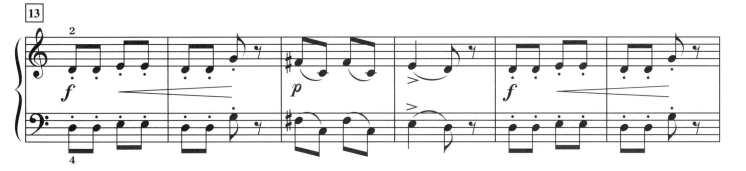

Dance

Ludvig Schytte (1848–1909)
Op. 108, No. 1

1-8 (40)

Keys of C Major and A Minor

Objectives

Upon completion of this unit the student will be able to:

1. Play the C major scale and arpeggio using traditional fingerings.
2. Build and play the primary chords in close position in the key of C major.
3. Sight-read music that uses the C major scale.
4. Aurally identify incorrect notes in the C major scale.
5. Play the A harmonic minor scale and arpeggio using traditional fingerings.
6. Build and play the primary chords in close position in the key of A minor.
7. Perform solo repertoire that uses primary chords in close position in the key of A minor.
8. Sight-read music that uses primary chords in the key of A minor.
9. Aurally distinguish i, iv and V7 chords in the key of A minor.
10. Harmonize a melody from a lead sheet that uses major and minor chords with block chord and broken chord accompaniment patterns.

Assignments

Week of _____

Write your assignments for the week in the space below.

_____

_____

_____

_____

_____

Did You Know?

George Frideric Handel and Domenico Scarlatti

George Frideric Handel

George Frideric Handel (1685–1759) and Domenico Scarlatti (1685–1757) were important composers in the Baroque period. Handel is most famous for his oratorio, Messiah, *but he also wrote other music including operas and orchestral works. Handel was born in Germany but lived much of his life in England where he held a dominant position in the musical life of the country. Scarlatti, an Italian, is remembered for writing more than 500 keyboard sonatas. Most of these sonatas are one-movement works, but many are arranged in pairs, sometimes similar in mood, and other times showing great contrast. Scarlatti combined interesting themes with rhythmic vitality to create highly idiomatic keyboard works.*

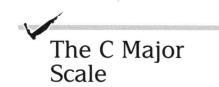

The C Major Scale

Remember that the major scale is made up of two tetrachords *joined* by a whole step. The 2nd tetrachord of the C major scale begins on G. There is no ♯ or ♭ in the C major scale.

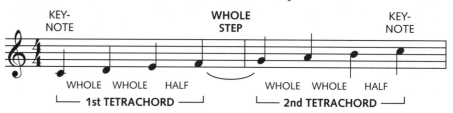

🔊 1-9 (41)   Play the C major scale hands separately.

The C Major Arpeggio

Play the C major arpeggio hands separately.

🔊 1-10 (42)

🔊 1-10 (42)

The Primary Chords in C Major

The three most important chords in any key are those built on the 1st, 4th & 5th notes of the scale. These are called the **primary chords** of the key.

The chords are identified by the Roman numerals **I, IV & V** (1, 4 & 5). The **V** chord usually adds the note a 7th above the root to make a **V7** (say "5-7") chord.

In the key of C major, the **I** chord is the C major triad. The **IV** chord is the F major triad. The **V7** chord is the G7 chord (G major triad with an added 7th).

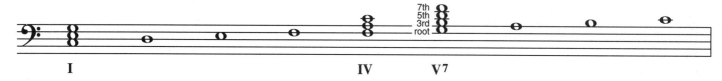

When we change from one chord to another, we call this a **chord progression.** When all chords are in root position, the hand must leap from one chord to the next. To make the chord progressions easier to play and sound better, the IV and V7 chords may be played in other positions by moving one or more of the higher chord tones down an octave. Chord progressions using these positions are often described as being in **close position.**

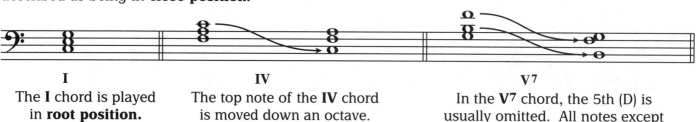

I
The **I** chord is played in **root position.**

IV
The top note of the **IV** chord is moved down an octave.

V7
In the **V7** chord, the 5th (D) is usually omitted. All notes except the root are moved down an octave.

◀))) **1-11 (43)**　　　　　　　Play the primary chords in C major.

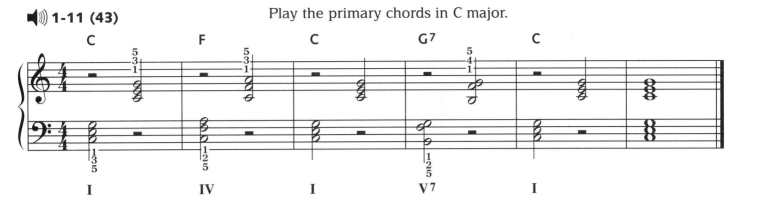

READING

Play the following example, counting aloud.

◀))) **1-12 (44)**

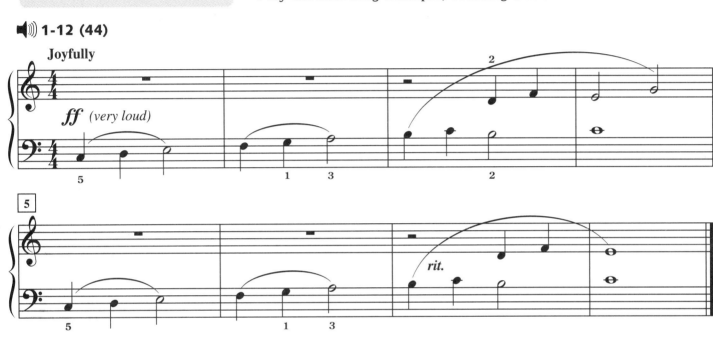

EAR TRAINING

Your teacher will play C major scales. One note in each scale will be played incorrectly. Circle the incorrect note.

Teacher: See page 145.

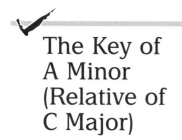

The Key of A Minor (Relative of C Major)

Every major key has a **relative minor key** that has the same key signature. The relative minor begins on the 6th tone of the major scale. The relative minor of C major is, therefore, A minor.

Because the keys of C major & A minor have the same key signature (no #'s, no ♭'s), they are **relatives.**

The minor scale shown below is called the **natural minor scale.** It uses only notes that are found in the relative major scale.

C MAJOR SCALE

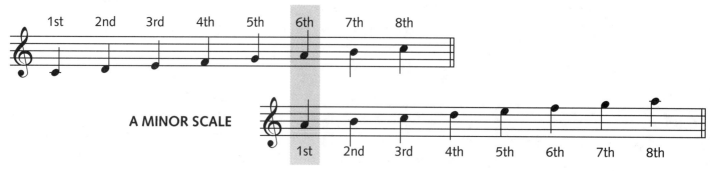

The A Harmonic Minor Scale

The most frequently used minor scale is the **harmonic minor.** In this scale, the 7th tone is raised ascending and descending.

The raised 7th in the key of A minor is G#. It is not included in the key signature, but is written in as an "accidental" sharp each time it occurs.

Practice slowly hands separately. Lean the hand slightly in the direction you are moving. The hand should move smoothly along with no twisting motion of the wrist.

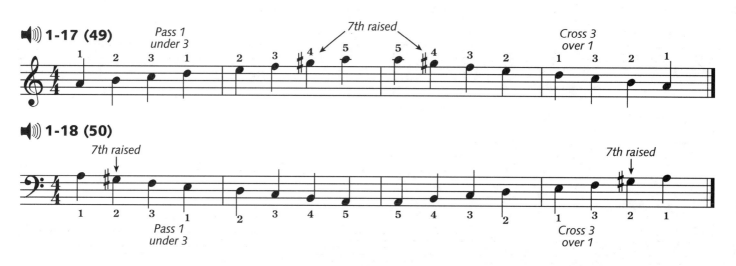

Play the scales above hands together. The RH ascends as the LH descends and vice versa (contrary motion). Both hands play the same numbered fingers at the same time.

The A Minor Arpeggio

Play the A minor arpeggio hands separately.

The Primary Chords in A Minor

In the key of A minor, the **i** chord is the A minor triad. The **iv** chord is the D minor triad. The **V7** chord is the E7 chord (E major triad with an added 7th). Note that the harmonic form of A minor is used.

Lower case Roman numerals are used to indicate minor triads (**i** & **iv**). (Lower case m = minor.)

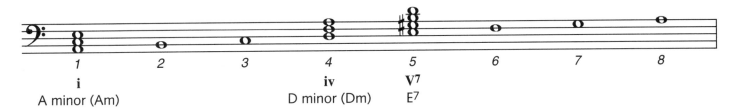

The following positions are often used, for smooth progressions.

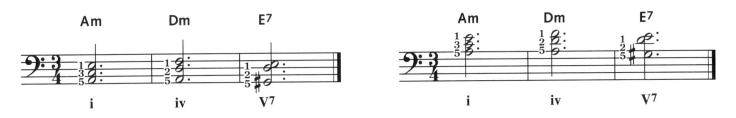

Play the primary chords in A minor.

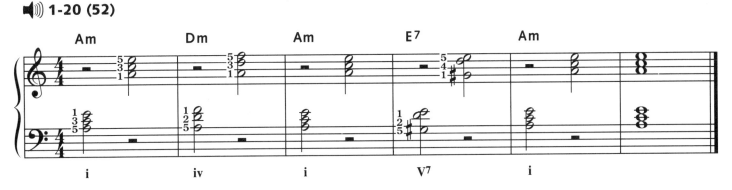

TECHNIQUE

SOLO REPERTOIRE

Go Down, Moses

🔊 **1-25 (57)**

Spiritual
arr. Kenon D. Renfrow

Moderately slow

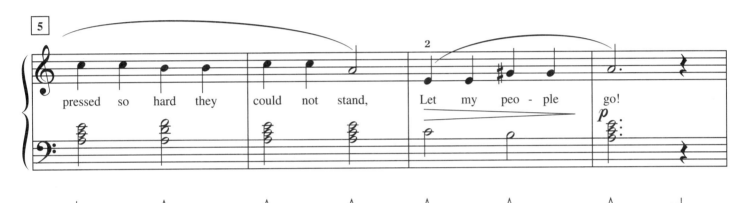

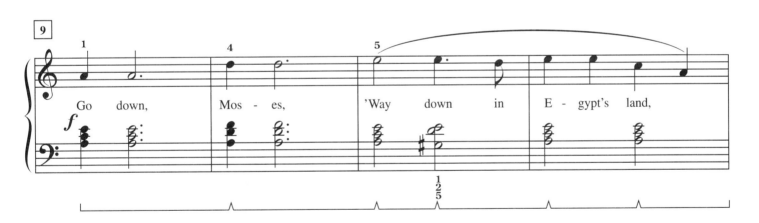

READING

Play the following example, counting aloud.

Moderately slow

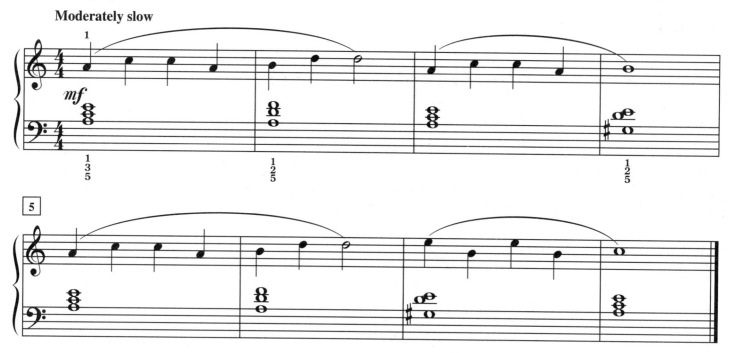

EAR TRAINING

Your teacher will play a chord progression.
Circle the progression that you hear.

a.

b.

c.

d.
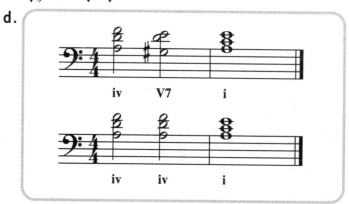

Teacher: See page 145.

20   Unit 2   ▓ Keys of C Major and A Minor

Harmonizing Melodies from a Lead Sheet

1. Using the indicated chords, harmonize the following melody by continuing the block chord accompaniment pattern given in measures 2 and 3.

Morning Has Broken

🔊 **1-31 (63)**

Gaelic Folk Melody

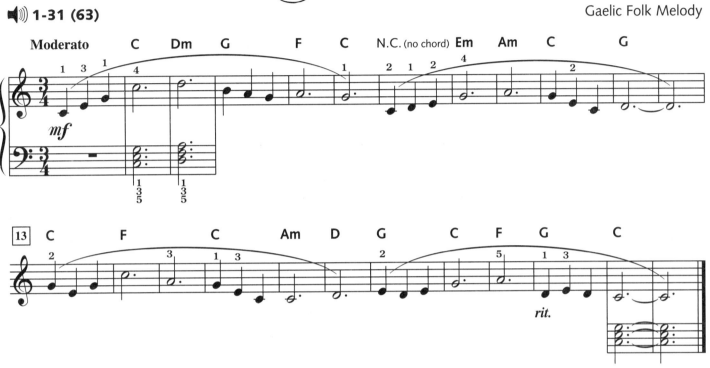

2. Using the indicated chords, harmonize the same melody by continuing the broken chord accompaniment pattern given in measures 2 and 3.

🔊 **1-32 (64)**

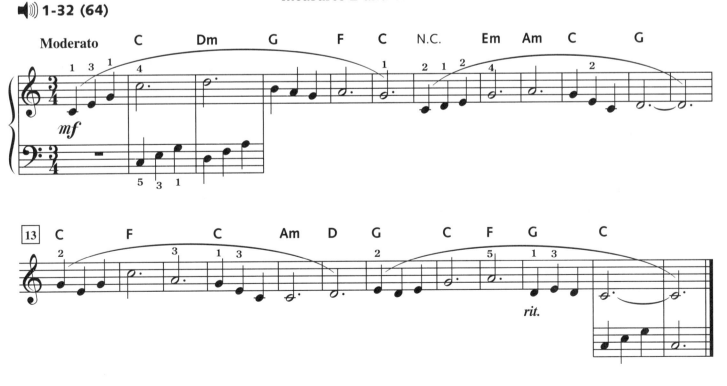

Keys of F Major and D Minor

UNIT THREE

Objectives

Upon completion of this unit the student will be able to:

1. Play the F major scale and arpeggio using traditional fingerings.
2. Build and play the primary chords in close position in the key of F major.
3. Sight-read music that uses primary chords in the key of F major.
4. Aurally identify melodic patterns in the key of F major.
5. Perform solo repertoire that uses primary chords in close position in the key of F major.
6. Play the D harmonic minor scale and arpeggio using traditional fingerings.
7. Build and play the primary chords in close position in the key of D minor.
8. Sight-read music that uses triads in the key of D minor.
9. Aurally distinguish i, iv and V7 chords in the key of D minor.

Assignments

Week of _____

Write your assignments for the week in the space below.

_____

_____

_____

_____

_____

_____

_____

_____

_____

Did You Know?

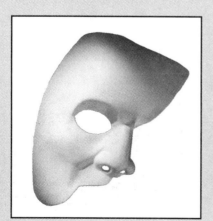

Opera and Musical Theatre

Opera can be best described as drama with music. It combines theatre, art, vocal music and instrumental music in an emotionally charged mixture. Operas can be comic (such as Strauss's Die Fledermaus*) or dramatic (such as Puccini's* Madame Butterfly*). Musical theatre or musical comedy developed in the United States during the late-nineteenth century. It is truly America's contribution to world theatre. Typically, musical theatre combines spoken dialogue, songs and dances. Andrew Lloyd Webber, a British composer, is the most commercially successful composer of his time. Among his hit shows are* Jesus Christ Superstar, Evita, Cats, Phantom of the Opera *and* Sunset Boulevard.

The F Major Scale

Remember that the major scale is made up of two tetrachords joined by a whole step. The 2nd tetrachord of the F major scale begins on C. There is one flat (B♭) in the F major scale.

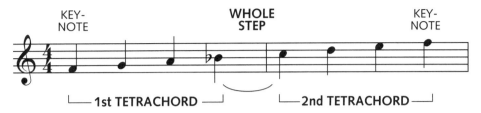

Play the F major scale hands separately.

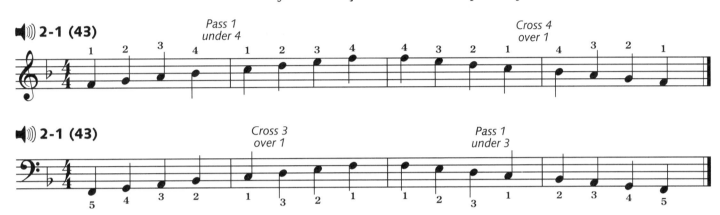

The F Major Arpeggio

Play the F major arpeggio hands separately.

The Primary Chords in F Major

Play the primary chords in F major.

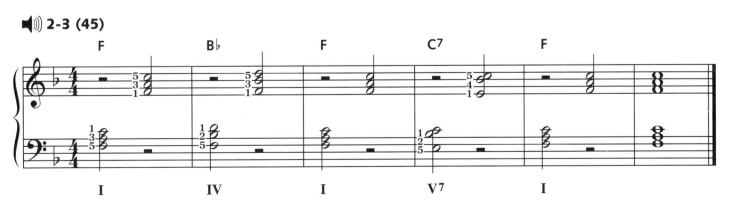

READING

Play the following example, counting aloud.

🔊 2-4 (46)

EAR TRAINING

Your teacher will play melodic patterns in the key of F major. Circle the melody that you hear.

🔊 2-5 (47)

a.

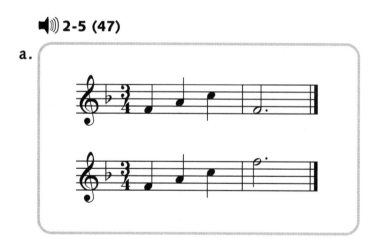

🔊 2-6 (48)

b.

🔊 2-7 (49)

c.

🔊 2-8 (50)

d.

Teacher: See page 145.

SOLO REPERTOIRE

Auld Lang Syne

Traditional
arr. Kenon D. Renfrow

2-9 (51)

Keys of F Major and D Minor Unit 3 **25**

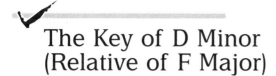

The Key of D Minor (Relative of F Major)

D minor is the relative of F major.

Both keys have the same key signature (1 flat, B♭).

Remember: The relative minor begins on the 6th tone of the major scale.

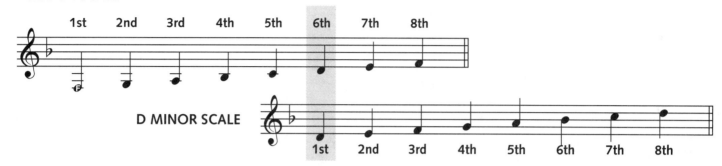

Play the D harmonic minor scale hands separately.

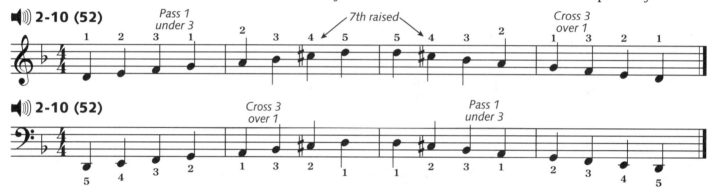

The D Minor Arpeggio

Play the D minor arpeggio hands separately.

The Primary Chords in D Minor

Play the primary chords in D minor.

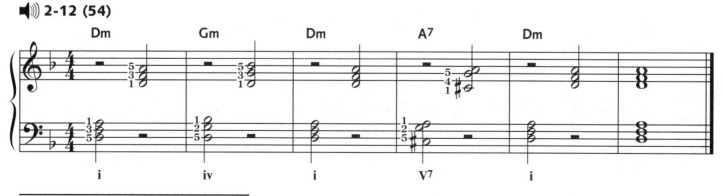

EAR TRAINING

Your teacher will play **i, iv** and **V7** chords in the key of D minor. Write the Roman numeral name for each chord. The first chord is shown.

🔊 **2-13 (55)**

a. <u>i</u>   ____   ____   ____

🔊 **2-14 (56)**

b. <u>iv</u>   ____   ____   ____

🔊 **2-15 (57)**

c. <u>iv</u>   ____   ____   ____

🔊 **2-16 (58)**

d. <u>i</u>   ____   ____   ____

Teacher: See page 145.

READING

Play the following example counting aloud.

🔊 **2-17 (59)**

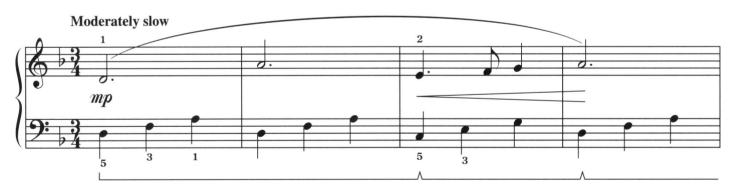

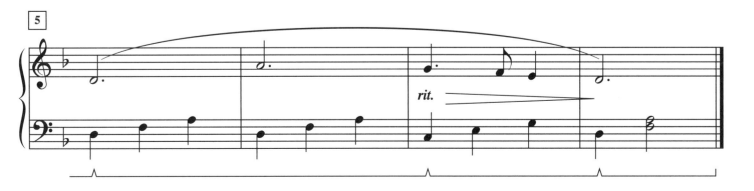

TECHNIQUE

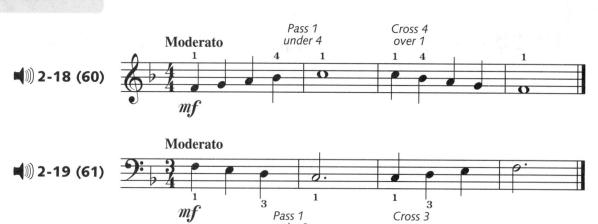

🔊 2-18 (60)

🔊 2-19 (61)

🔊 2-20 (62)

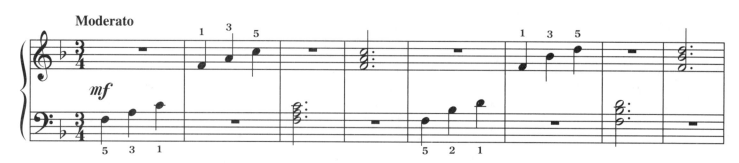

🔊 2-21 (63)

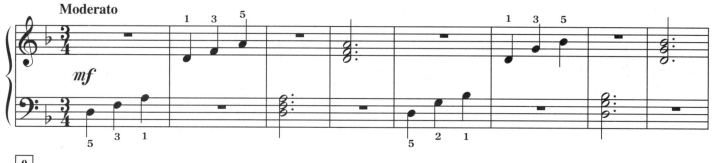

$\frac{6}{8}$ Time Signature

Objectives

Upon completion of this unit the student will be able to:

1. Identify $\frac{6}{8}$ time signature and apply it to performance at the keyboard.
2. Clap or tap rhythms in $\frac{6}{8}$ time.
3. Play melodies in $\frac{6}{8}$ time.
4. Perform solo repertoire in $\frac{6}{8}$ time.
5. Tap two-part rhythm patterns.
6. Sight-read music in $\frac{6}{8}$ time.
7. Aurally identify rhythm patterns in $\frac{6}{8}$ time.
8. Perform ensemble repertoire with partners.

Assignments

Week of _____

Write your assignments for the week in the space below.

_____

_____

_____

_____

_____

_____

_____

_____

_____

_____

Did You Know?

Franz Joseph Haydn

*F*ranz Joseph Haydn (1732–1809) was born in Austria and spent most of his life near Vienna. For thirty years he was employed by Prince Nikolaus Esterhazy, one of the richest and most influential Hungarian nobles. Haydn matured slowly as a composer, yet his musical output was vast. He wrote over 100 symphonies, more than 40 piano sonatas, over 20 operas, numerous string quartets and trios, and many masses and songs. His oratorio, The Creation, has been compared to Handel's Messiah. Haydn's philosophy of life was to be good and industrious while serving God continually.

A New Time Signature

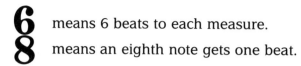

6 means 6 beats to each measure.
8 means an eighth note gets one beat.

Clap (or tap) the following rhythms.
Clap once for each note, counting aloud.

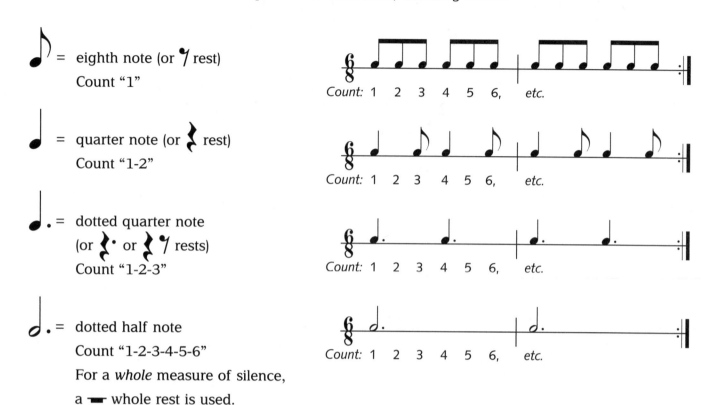

♪ = eighth note (or ⅞ rest)
Count "1"

♩ = quarter note (or 𝄽 rest)
Count "1-2"

♩. = dotted quarter note
(or 𝄽· or 𝄽⅞ rests)
Count "1-2-3"

𝅗𝅥. = dotted half note
Count "1-2-3-4-5-6"
For a *whole* measure of silence,
a ▬ whole rest is used.

RHYTHM READING

Clap (or tap) the following rhythms, counting aloud.

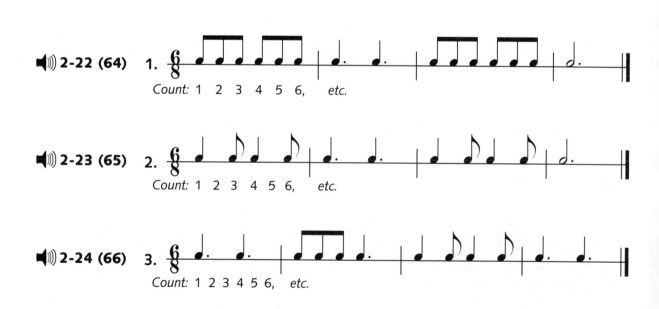

2-22 (64) 1.

2-23 (65) 2.

2-24 (66) 3.

READING

Play each of these melodies in $\frac{6}{8}$ time, counting aloud.

Mexican Hat Dance

Allegro

Traditional

La Raspa

2-26 (68)

Allegro

Mexico

When Johnny Comes Marching Home

2-27 (69)

American Folk Song

March tempo

SOLO REPERTOIRE

*Respectfully dedicated to the
world-renowned concert pianist,
Vladimir Horowitz*

Scherzo*

Willard A. Palmer
Morton Manus
Amanda Vick Lethco

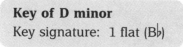

Key of D minor
Key signature: 1 flat (B♭)

Key of F major
(relative of D minor)

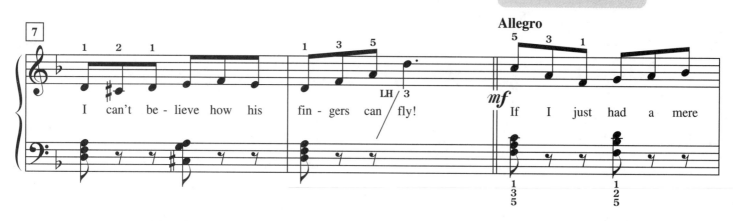

*Scherzo. This word means "a musical jest or joke." It is often applied to light and playful pieces.

10 por - tion of Vlad - i - mir Hor - o - witz' tal - ent I'd prac - tice all day!

Key of D minor

13 p I've a sus - pi - cion it's more than am - bi - tion, it's how man - y D. C. al

16 fi - nes you play. mf May - be to - mor - row it's Vlad - i - mir Hor - o - witz

*accelerando poco a poco al fine**
Both hands 8va - - - - - - - - - - - - - -

19 who'll be ap - plaud - ing the mu - sic I play. f **Pres - to, pres - tis - si - mo.

(Both hands 8va) -

22 ***Brav - o, brav - is - si - mo! I'm get - ting bet - ter and bet - ter each day! LH 3

* *Accelerando poco a poco al fine.* Gradually faster little by little to the end.

** *Presto.* Italian for "fast." This tempo mark means "faster than allegro."
   The word *prestissimo* means "very fast." It usually means "as fast as possible."

*** *Bravo, bravissimo!* These Italian words are often shouted by audiences of virtuoso performers.
   They can't be exactly translated, but they mean something like "Marvelous, *very* marvelous!"

READING

RHYTHM READING

Tap the following rhythm patterns using RH for notes with stems going up and LH for notes with stems going down. Tap hands separately first, and then hands together, always counting aloud.

EAR TRAINING

1. Your teacher will clap a rhythm pattern.
   Circle the pattern that you hear.

🔊 **2-34 (76)**

a.

🔊 **2-35 (77)**

1b.

🔊 **2-36 (78)**

c.
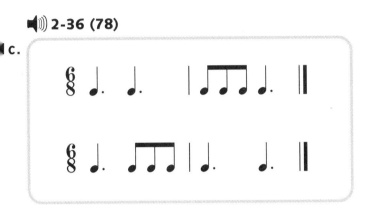

🔊 **2-37 (79)**

1d.

2. Your teacher will clap a rhythm pattern.
   Draw the missing notes in the second measure using ♩. ♩. ♩ 𝅘𝅥𝅮𝅘𝅥𝅮𝅘𝅥𝅮 or ♪

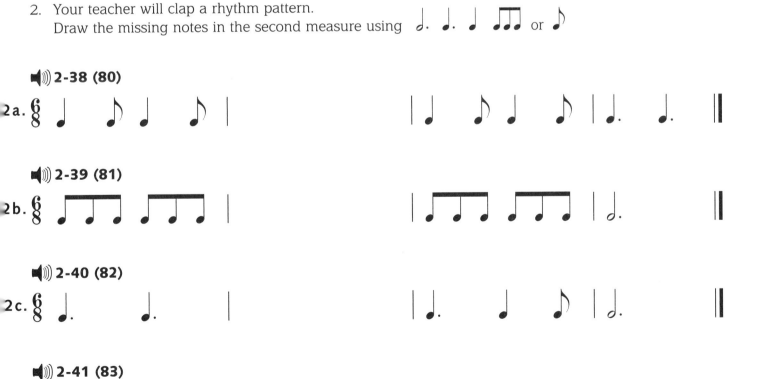

🔊 **2-38 (80)**

2a.

🔊 **2-39 (81)**

2b.

🔊 **2-40 (82)**

2c.

🔊 **2-41 (83)**

2d.

Teacher: See page 145.

Take Me Out to the Ball Game

🔊 2-42 (84)

Albert von Tilzer

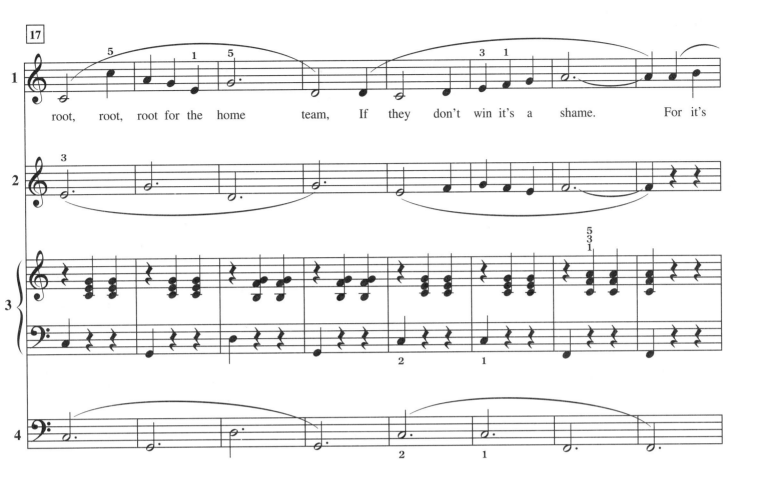

root, root, root for the home team, If they don't win it's a shame. For it's

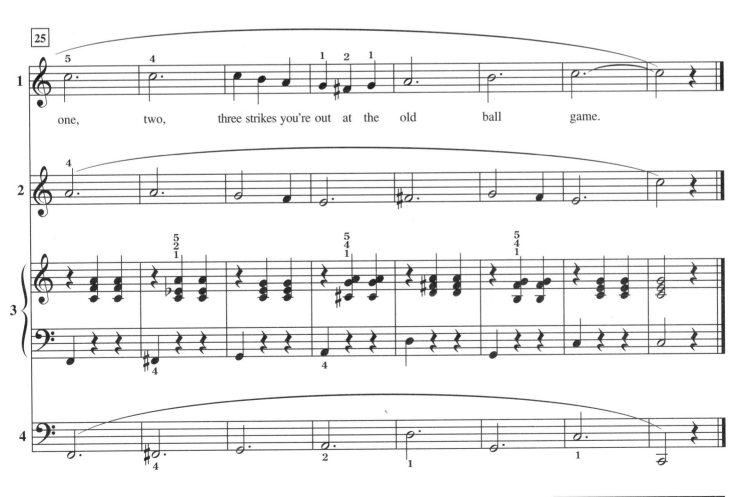

one, two, three strikes you're out at the old ball game. For it's

Keys of G Major and E Minor

Objectives

Upon completion of this unit the student will be able to:

1. Play the G major scale and arpeggio using traditional fingerings.
2. Build and play the primary chords in close position in the key of G major.
3. Perform solo repertoire that uses primary chords in close position in the key of G major.
4. Tap two-part rhythm patterns.
5. Play the E harmonic minor scale and arpeggio using traditional fingerings.
6. Build and play the primary chords in close position in the key of E minor.
7. Sight-read music that uses triads in the key of E minor.
8. Aurally distinguish i, iv and V7 chords in the key of E minor.

Assignments

Week of _____

Write your assignments for the week in the space below.

_____

_____

_____

_____

_____

_____

_____

_____

Did You Know?

Symphony Orchestra

Today the term "orchestra" usually refers to a symphony orchestra consisting mainly of string instruments. Symphony orchestras also have woodwind, brass and percussion instruments. Symphony orchestras were organized in France and Italy during the late 16th century and early 17th century. Orchestras were small until the early 19th century and were performed without a conductor. Among the first conductors of large orchestras were composers Hector Berlioz and Felix Mendelssohn. Popular types of orchestral music include symphonies, overtures and concertos. A symphony is a large-scale musical composition divided into sections called movements. Most symphonies have four movements, but some have only one while others have as many as six.

The G Major Scale

Remember that the major scale is made up of two tetrachords *joined* by a whole step. The 2nd tetrachord of the G major scale begins on D. There is 1 sharp (F♯) in the G major scale.

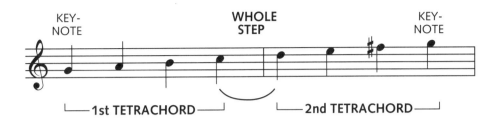

Play the G major scale hands separately.

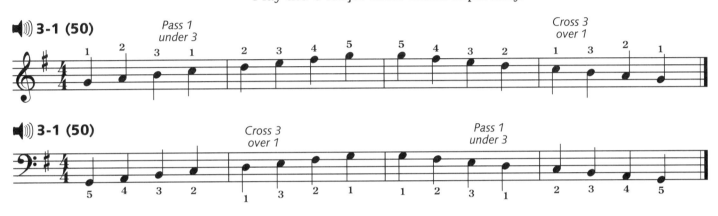

The G Major Arpeggio

Play the G major arpeggio hands separately.

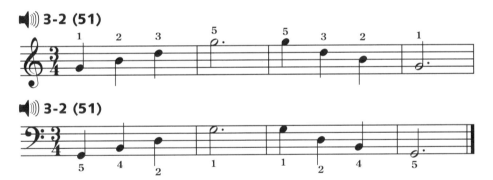

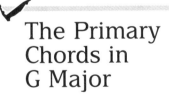

The Primary Chords in G Major

Play the primary chords in G major.

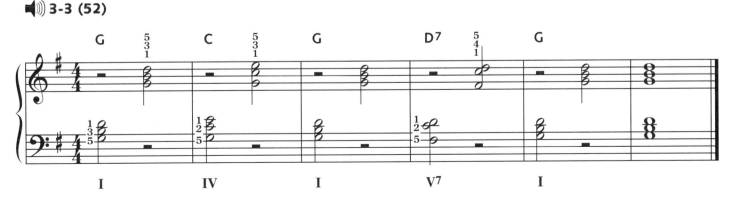

RHYTHM READING

Tap the following rhythm patterns using RH for notes with stems going up and LH for notes with stems going down. Tap hands separately first, and then hands together, always counting aloud.

🔊 3-4 (53)

1.

🔊 3-5 (54)

2.

🔊 3-6 (55)

3.

SOLO REPERTOIRE

Nobody Knows the Trouble I've Seen

🔊 3-7 (56)

Spiritual
arr. Kenon D. Renfrow

Adagio

No-bod-y knows the trou-ble I've seen, No-bod-y knows my sor-row!

No-bod-y knows the trou-ble I've seen, Glo-ry hal-le-lu-jah! Some-

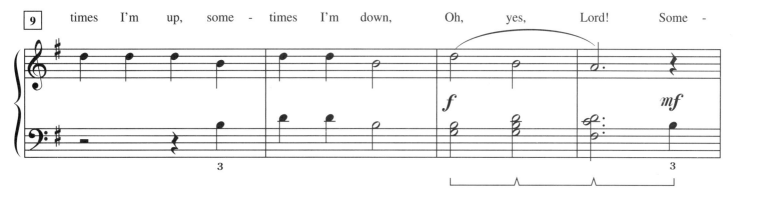

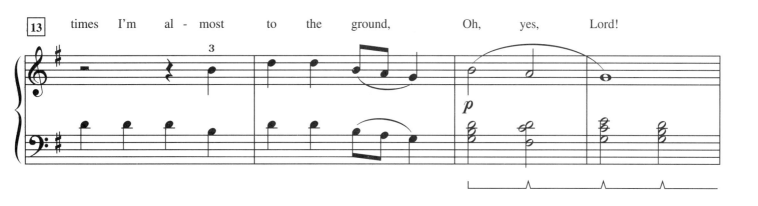

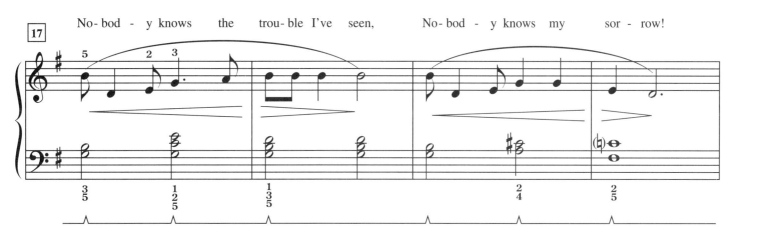

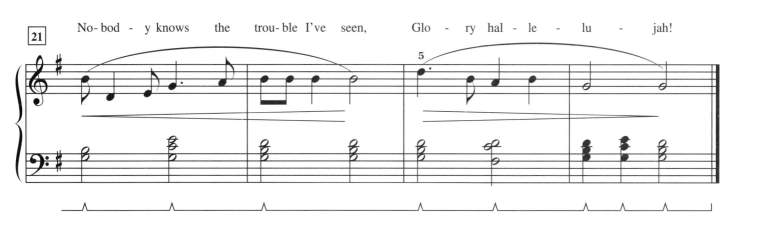

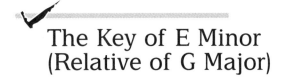

The Key of E Minor (Relative of G Major)

E minor is the relative of G major.

Both keys have the same key signature (1 sharp, F#).

Remember: The relative minor begins on the 6th tone of the major scale.

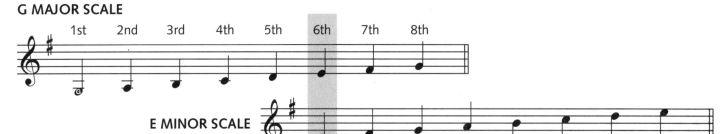

Play the E harmonic minor scale hands separately.

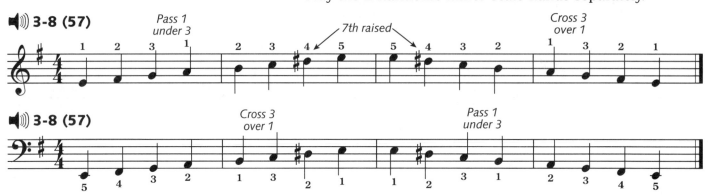

The E Minor Arpeggio

Play the E minor arpeggio hands separately.

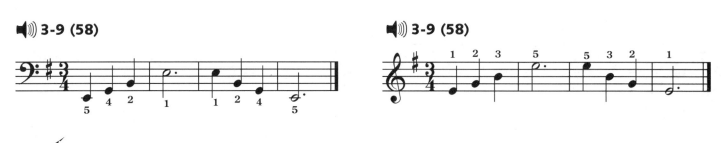

The Primary Chords in E Minor

Play the primary chords in E minor.

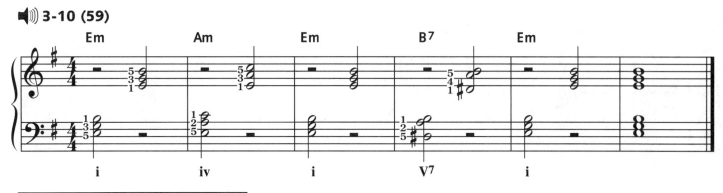

EAR TRAINING

Your teacher will play i, iv and V7 chords in the key of E minor. Write the Roman numeral name for each chord. The first chord is shown.

🔊 **3-11 (60)**

a. i ____ ____ ____

🔊 **3-12 (61)**

b. iv ____ ____ ____

🔊 **3-13 (62)**

c. V⁷ ____ ____ ____

🔊 **3-14 (63)**

d. iv ____ ____ ____

Teacher: See page 146.

READING

Play the following example, counting aloud.

🔊 **3-15 (64)**

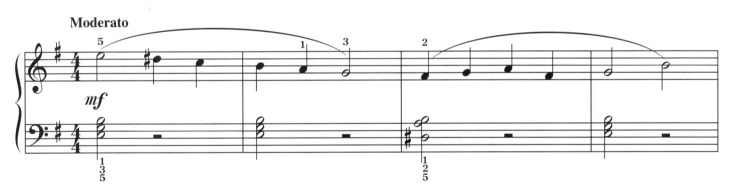

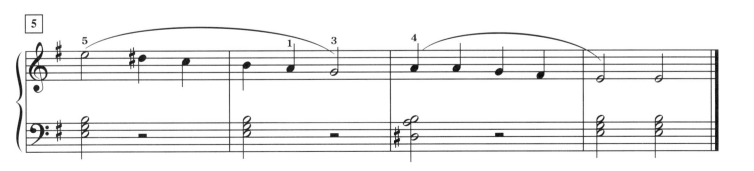

Alexander's Ragtime Band

Irving Berlin (1888–1989)
arr. E. L. Lancaster

🔊 3-16 (65)

Moderately

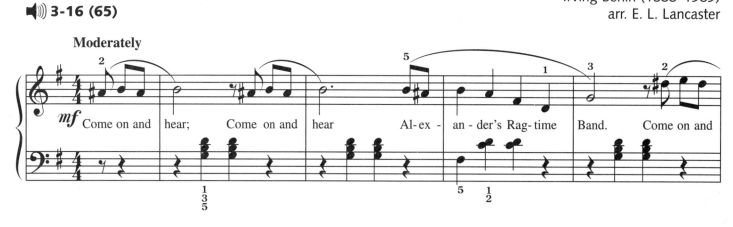

mf Come on and hear; Come on and hear Al-ex - an - der's Rag-time Band. Come on and

hear, Come on and hear, It's the best band in the land. They can

play a bu-gle call like you nev-er heard be-fore, So nat-ur-al that you want to go to war.

That's just the best-est band what am, Hon-ey Lamb, Come on a -

long,   Come on a - long,   Let me   take   you   by   the   hand,   Up   to   the

man,   up   to   the   man   who's   the   lead - er   of   the   band,   And   if   you

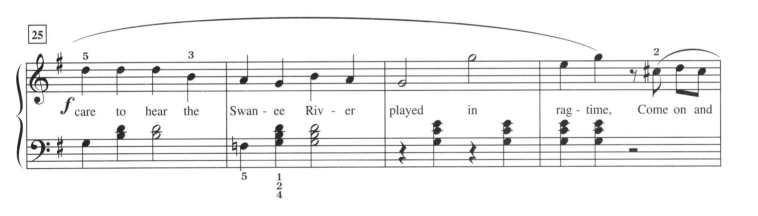

care   to   hear   the   Swan - ee   Riv - er   played   in   rag - time,   Come   on   and

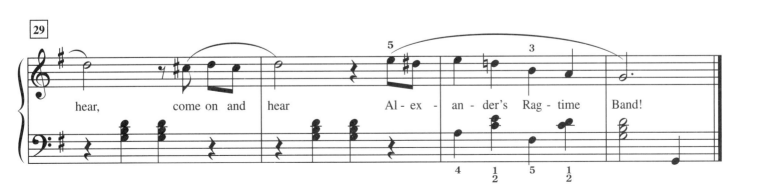

hear,   come   on   and   hear   Al - ex - an - der's   Rag - time   Band!

TECHNIQUE

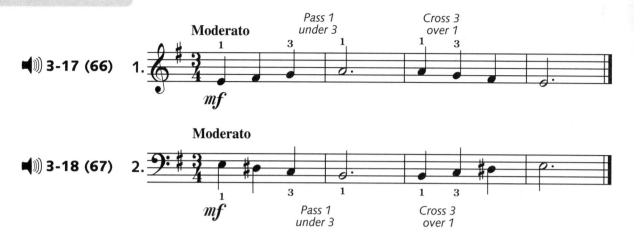

3-17 (66) 1.

3-18 (67) 2.

3-19 (68)

3.

3-20 (69)

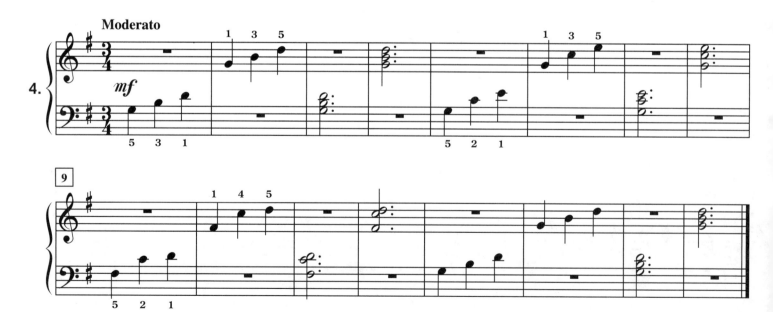

4.

Review Worksheet

Name _____   Date _____

1. Identify each chord in the key of E minor as i, iv or V7 by writing its name on the line.

_____   _____   _____   _____   _____   _____

2. Identify each chord in the key of F major as I, IV or V7 by writing its name on the line.

_____   _____   _____   _____   _____   _____

3. Identify each scale below by writing its name on the indicated line. Write the correct RH fingering on the line above the staff and the correct LH fingering on the line below the staff.

_____ minor

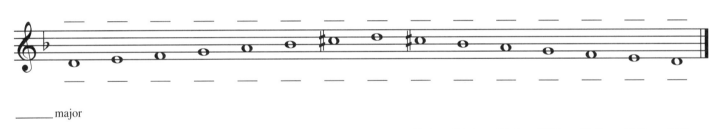

_____ major

4. Draw one note (𝅘𝅥𝅭 𝅘𝅥 or 𝅘𝅥𝅮) in each box to complete the measures.

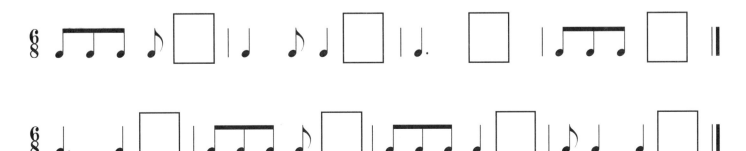

Key of D Major

Objectives

Upon completion of this unit the student will be able to:

1. Play the D major scale and arpeggio using traditional fingerings.
2. Build and play the primary chords in close position in the key of D major.
3. Sight-read music that uses primary chords in the key of D major.
4. Aurally identify incorrect notes in the D major scale.
5. Aurally distinguish I, IV and V7 chords in the key of D major.
6. Perform solo repertoire in the key of D major.

Assignments

Week of _____

Write your assignments for the week in the space below.

_____

_____

_____

_____

_____

_____

_____

_____

_____

_____

Did You Know?

Ludwig van Beethoven

Ludwig van Beethoven (1770–1827) bridged the gap between the Classical period and the Romantic period. Beethoven was born in Bonn, yet spent much of his life in Vienna. Beethoven was committed to imposing his will on the world through his music. Biographers often describe his horrible disposition, unconventional lack of manners and disgruntled appearance. Yet his works generally are regarded as musical masterpieces. Among his works are nine symphonies, five piano concertos, 16 string quartets, 32 piano sonatas, two masses, ten overtures, 10 sonatas for violin and piano, five sonatas for cello and piano, a violin concerto, an opera and numerous miscellaneous works. When his ninth symphony was performed in 1824 in Vienna, Beethoven was already deaf. On the platform with his back to the audience, he was unaware of their response until he turned and saw the enthusiastic applause.

The D Major Scale

Remember that the major scale is made up of two tetrachords joined by a whole step. The second tetrachord of the D major scale begins on A.

There are two sharps (F♯, C♯) in the D major scale.

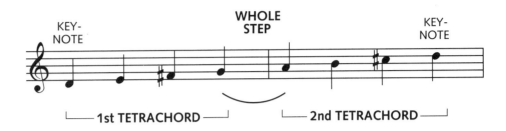

TECHNIQUE

🔊 **3-21 (70)**

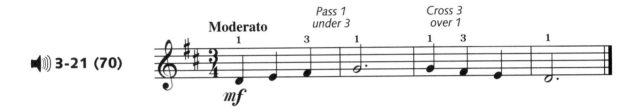

🔊 **3-22 (71)**

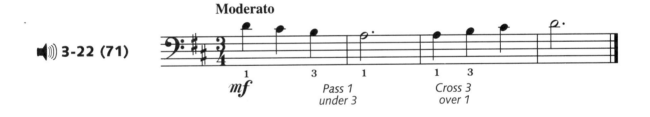

Play the D major scale hands separately.

🔊 **3-23 (72)**

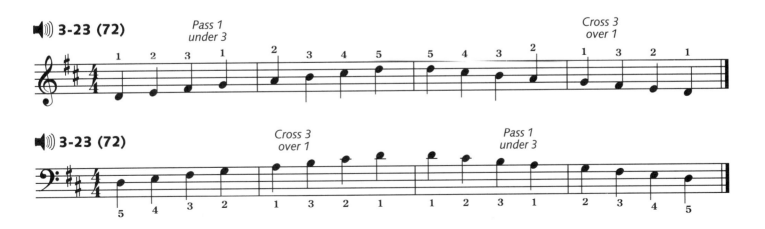

🔊 **3-23 (72)**

The D Major Arpeggio

Play the D major arpeggio hands separately.

🔊 3-24 (73)

🔊 3-24 (73)

The Primary Chords in D Major

Play the primary chords in D major.

🔊 3-25 (74)

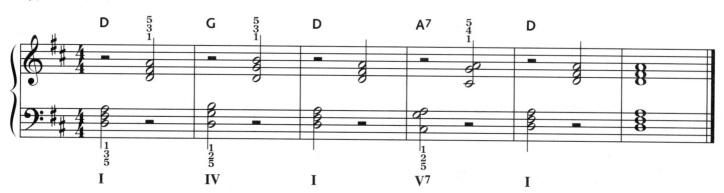

TECHNIQUE

🔊 3-26 (75)

READING

Play the following examples, counting aloud.

🔊 3-27 (76)

Allegro

1.

5

🔊 3-28 (77)

Moderato

2.

5

EAR TRAINING

1. Your teacher will play D major scales. One note of each scale will be played incorrectly. Circle the incorrect note.

🔊 **3-29 (78)**

1a.

🔊 **3-30 (79)**

1b.

🔊 **3-31 (80)**

1c.

🔊 **3-32 (81)**

1d.

2. Your teacher will play I, IV or V7 chords in the key of D. Circle the chords that you hear.

🔊 **3-33 (82)**

2a.

🔊 **3-34 (83)**

2b.

🔊 **3-35 (84)**

2c.

🔊 **3-36 (85)**

2d.

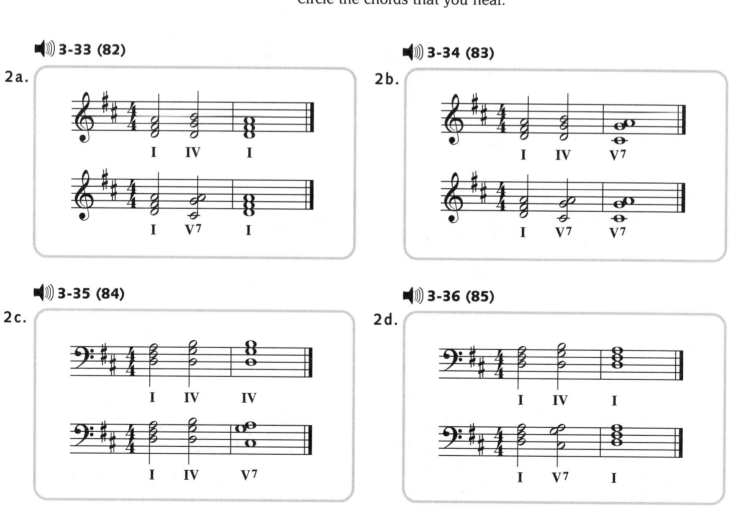

Teacher: See page 146.

Turkish March

from *The Ruins of Athens*

Ludwig van Beethoven (1770–1827)
Op. 113
arr. E. L. Lancaster

3-37 (86)

Allegretto

Triads and Inversions

Objectives

Upon completion of this unit the student will be able to:

1. Play triads in root position, first inversion and second inversion.
2. Sight-read music that uses triads, inversions and Alberti bass accompaniment patterns.
3. Perform solo repertoire that uses triads and inversions.

Assignments

Week of _____

Write your assignments for the week in the space below.

_____

_____

_____

_____

_____

_____

_____

_____

_____

_____

_____

_____

Did You Know?

The Piano Sonata

*The piano sonata has been one of the most favored genres for keyboard composition from the Classical period forward. Although the term came into use in the late 16th century to differentiate between instrumental and vocal music (as opposed to cantata, for vocal music), it has come to be known as any piece whose first movement follows the form exposition—development—recapitulation. In the **exposition,** the first theme is presented in the tonic key of the piece. Once this theme is well-established, a second theme is presented, usually in a different key. The **development** uses the thematic material presented in the exposition as a point of departure for altering and expanding those themes in many ways. In the **recapitulation,** the composer restates the exposition, with both themes now in the original key of the piece. Composers throughout time have experimented with new ways to alter the form, but the basic characteristics of sonata form have remained intact. Among the most familiar composers of piano sonatas are Franz Joseph Haydn, Wolfgang Amadeus Mozart, Ludwig van Beethoven and Sergei Prokofiev.*

Triads: First Inversion

When the root of the chord is moved to the top and the third becomes the lowest note of the triad, it is said to be in the **first inversion.**

C E G becomes E G C

The root is always the top note of the interval of a 4th.

 **3-38 (87)**

Play the following first-inversion triads in the key of C with RH, using 1 2 5 on each triad. Repeat with LH one octave lower, using 5 3 1 on each triad.

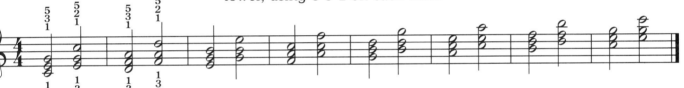

► Transpose to the keys of G major and F major.

 **3-39 (88)**

Play the following root position and first inversion triads with the RH, using the indicated fingering. Repeat with the LH one octave lower, using 5 3 1 on each triad.

READING

Play the following example, counting aloud.

3-40 (89)

Triads: Second Inversion

Any first-inversion triad may be inverted again by moving the lowest note to the top. All letter names are the same, but the root is in the middle and the fifth is the lowest note of the triad. This is called the **second inversion.**

E G C becomes G C E

The root is always the top note of the interval of a 4th.

🔊 **3-41 (90)**

Play the following second-inversion triads in the key of C with LH, using 5 2 1 on each triad. Repeat with RH one octave higher, using 1 3 5 on each triad.

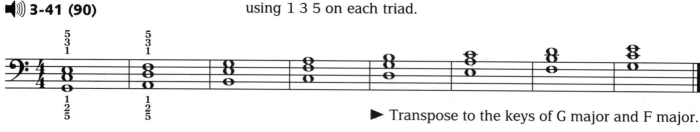

▶ Transpose to the keys of G major and F major.

READING

Play the following example, counting aloud.

🔊 **3-42 (91)**

Slow march tempo

Triads: All Positions

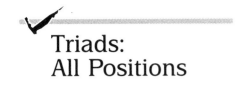

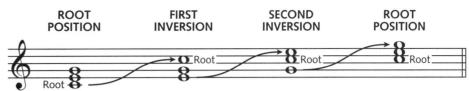

Play the following:

3-43 (92)

1.

► Transpose to the keys of G major and F major.

3-43 (92)

2.

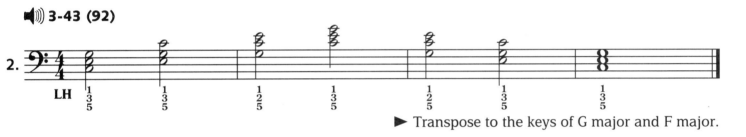

► Transpose to the keys of G major and F major.

Naming Triads and Inversions

Roman numerals identify the scale degrees on which triads are built within a key.

Numbers to the right of the Roman numerals indicate the intervals between the lowest note and each of the other notes of the chord.

In the first inversion, the number 3 is usually omitted.

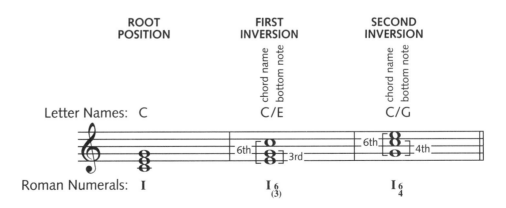

READING

Play the following examples, counting aloud.

🔊 3-44 (93)

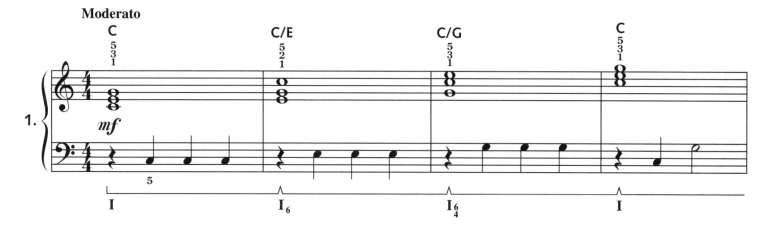

🔊 3-45 (94)

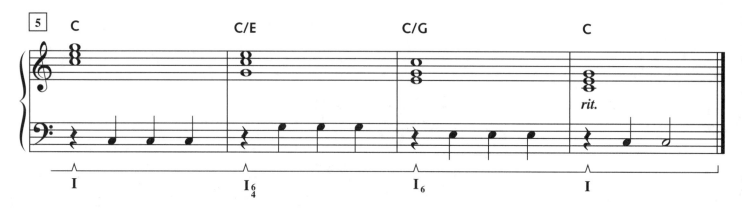

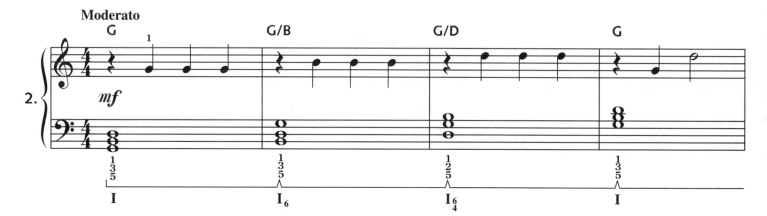

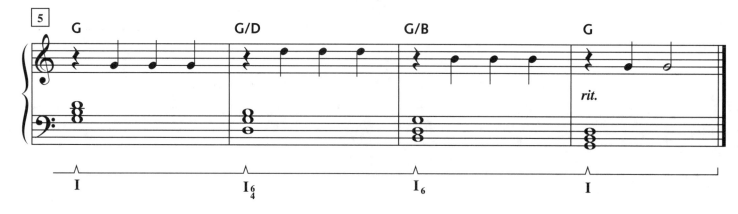

Simile as used in this piece means to continue pedal in the same manner.

Etude

3-46 (95)

Ludvig Schytte
(1848–1909)

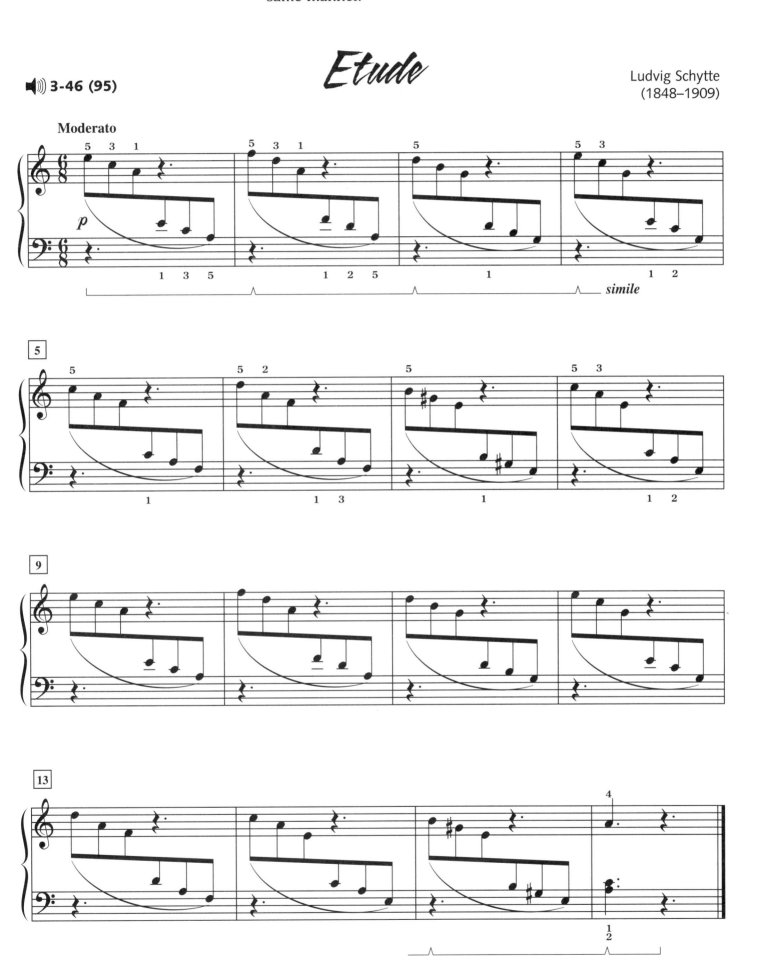

Alberti Bass Accompaniment

Chords are often used as follows:

BLOCK CHORD

ALBERTI BASS

bottom   top   middle   top

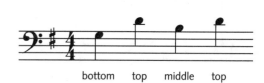

bottom   top   middle   top

TECHNIQUE

🔊 **3-47 (96)**

Moderato

1.

🔊 **3-48 (97)**

Moderato

2.

READING

Play the following examples, counting aloud.

🔊 3-49 (98)

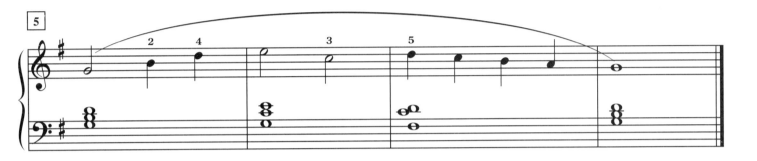

🔊 3-49 (98)

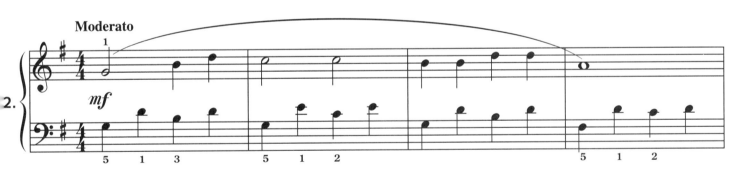

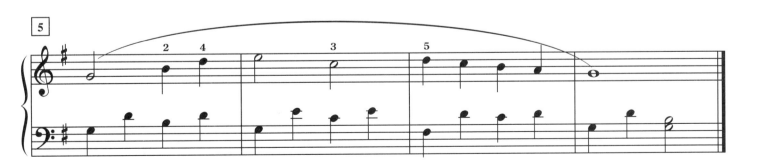

Augmented and Diminished Triads

Objectives

Upon completion of this unit the student will be able to:

1. Play major, minor, augmented and diminished chords.
2. Harmonize a melody from a lead sheet that uses chords and inversions.
3. Perform solo repertoire that uses augmented triads and eighth-note triplets.
4. Clap or tap rhythm patterns that use eighth-note triplets.
5. Sight-read music that uses eighth-note triplets.
6. Aurally identify rhythm patterns with eighth-note triplets.

Assignments

Week of _____

Write your assignments for the week in the space below.

_____

_____

_____

_____

_____

_____

_____

_____

_____

_____

_____

_____

Did You Know?

Franz Schubert

Although widely known as a composer of vocal music called lieder, *Franz Schubert (1797–1828) also composed 22 piano sonatas and many short piano pieces for two and four hands. He was educated to follow in his father's footsteps as a school teacher, but after a brief time, he abandoned teaching to pursue his passion—musical composition. Schubert's music is characterized by gorgeous melodies accompanied by a complex harmonic vocabulary. Schubert preferred to present his music in intimate settings, usually in private homes. These performances, known as Schubertiads, were held once a week for several years. Schubert was one of the first musicians to earn his living solely from the sale of his music. Like so many others, Schubert died young, at the age of 31, as a result of struggling constantly against illness and poverty.*

Augmented Chords

A major chord becomes **augmented** when the fifth is raised a half step. A plus sign (+) indicates an augmented chord.

C Major Chord

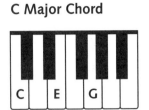

C Augmented Chord

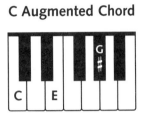

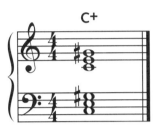

Playing Major and Augmented Chords

Play the following exercise that uses major (M) and augmented (A) chords.

 4-1 (49)

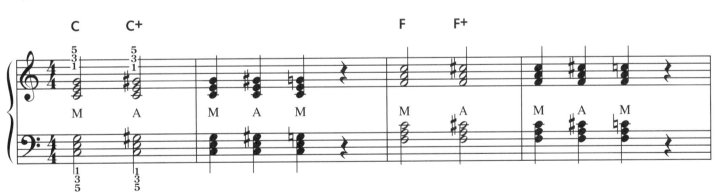

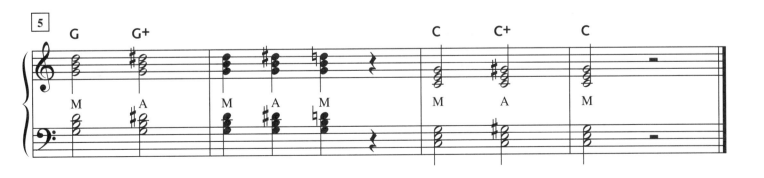

Diminished Chords

A minor chord becomes **diminished** when the fifth is lowered a half step. A small circle (°) indicates a diminished chord.

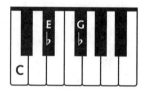

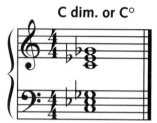

Playing Minor and Diminished Chords

Play the following exercise that uses minor (m) and diminished (d) chords.

4-2 (50)

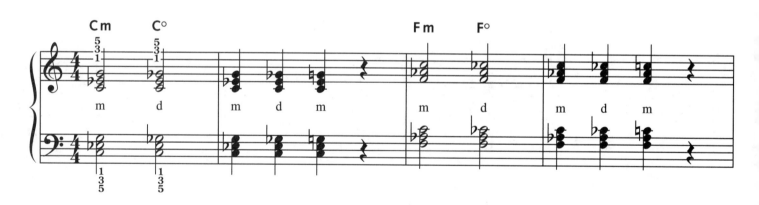

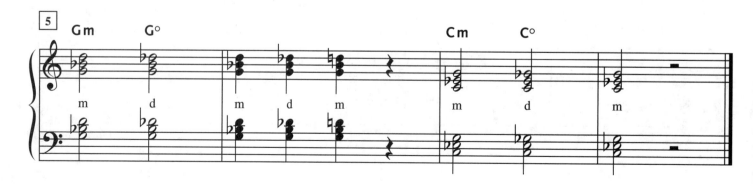

Harmonizing Melodies from a Lead Sheet

Using the indicated chords, harmonize the following melody by continuing the broken-chord accompaniment pattern given in the first two measures.

Just a Closer Walk

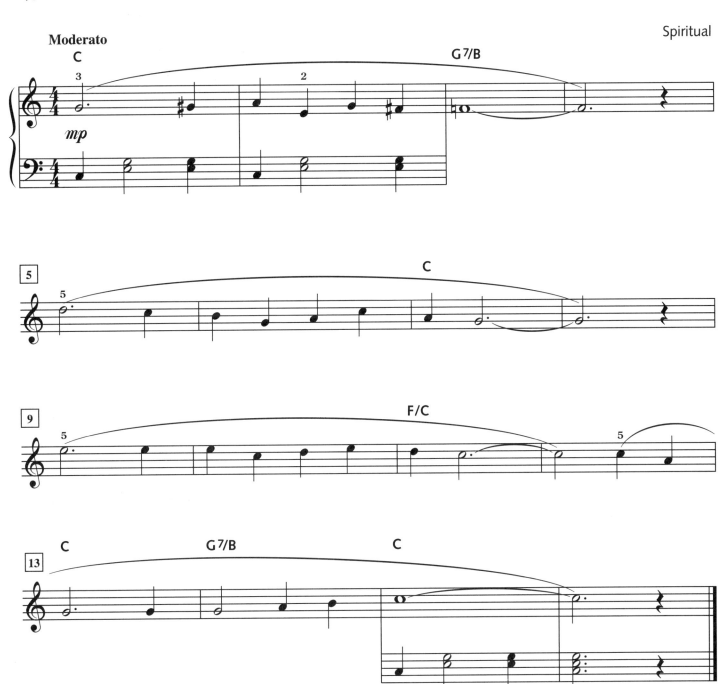

Theme from Symphony No. 9

(From the New World)

🔊 **4-4 (52)**

Antonin Dvořák (1841–1904)
arr. E. L. Lancaster

Largo (very slow)

Eighth-Note Triplets

When three notes are grouped together with a figure "3" above or below the notes, the group is called a **triplet.** The three notes of an eighth-note triplet group equal one quarter note.

When a piece contains triplets, count "trip-a-let" or "1-and-a."

RHYTHM READING

Clap or tap the following rhythms, counting aloud.

Etude

🔊 4-10 (58)

Cornelius Gurlitt
(1820–1901)

EAR TRAINING

Your teacher will clap a rhythm pattern. Draw the missing notes in the third measure, using

Teacher: See page 146.

READING

Play the following example, counting aloud.

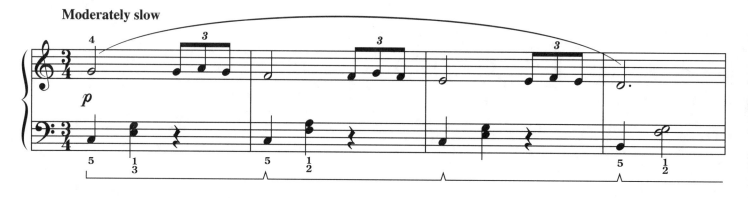

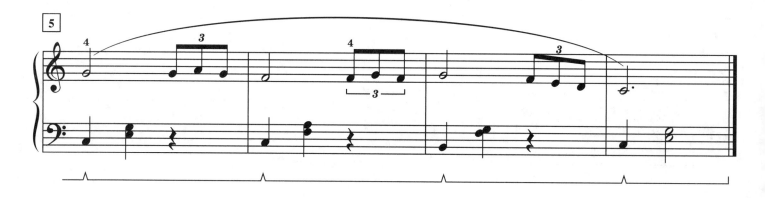

Sixteenth Notes

Objectives

Upon completion of this unit the student will be able to:

1. Clap or tap rhythm patterns that use sixteenth notes.
2. Perform solo repertoire that uses sixteenth notes.
3. Aurally identify rhythm patterns that use sixteenth notes and dotted eighth notes.
4. Sight-read music that uses sixteenth notes and dotted eighth notes.
5. Tap two-part rhythm patterns.
6. Perform duet repertoire with a partner.

Assignments

Week of _____

Write your assignments for the week in the space below.

_____

_____

_____

_____

_____

_____

_____

_____

_____

_____

_____

_____

Did You Know?

Johannes Brahms and Robert Schumann

Robert Schumann

Johannes Brahms (1833–1897) and Robert Schumann (1810–1856) were major composers of the Romantic period. Brahms, himself a child prodigy, wrote in a style all his own. He began performing publicly at an early age and through this was exposed to a vast amount of music. Schumann also showed much musical promise as a child, but his parents wanted him to pursue a more noble career. After attending law school for a short while, Robert forsook school to be a musician. He had already established a successful career in music when he met Brahms. After hearing some of Brahms's music, Schumann immediately declared Brahms a genius. The two were close friends until Schumann's death in 1856.

Sixteenth Notes

When a sixteenth note is written alone it has two flags (♬).

When written in pairs or groups of four, they are joined with two beams (♬ ♬♬).

Four sixteenth notes are played in the time of one quarter note:

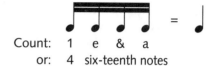

Count: 1 e & a
or: 4 six-teenth notes

READING

Clap (or tap) the following rhythms, counting aloud.

🔊 4-16 (64)

1. 1 e & a 2 & etc.

🔊 4-17 (65)

2. 1 e & 2 e & etc.

🔊 4-18 (66)

3. 1 & a 2 & etc.

🔊 4-19 (67)

4. 1 e & a 2 e & etc.

🔊 4-20 (68)

5. 1 2 & etc.

SOLO REPERTOIRE

Theme from Rondo a Capriccio

(Rage over the Lost Penny)

Ludwig van Beethoven (1770–1827)
arr. E. L. Lancaster

🔊 4-21 (69)

EAR TRAINING

Your teacher will clap a rhythm pattern. Draw the missing notes in the second measure, using  or

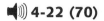 4-22 (70)

a.

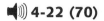 4-23 (71)

b.

 4-24 (72)

c.

 4-25 (73)

d.

Teacher: See page 146.

READING

Play the following example, counting aloud.

 4-26 (74)

Dotted Eighth Notes

A dotted eighth note has the same value as an eighth note tied to a sixteenth note.

Count aloud and play:

The following line should sound exactly the same as the above line. The only difference is the way it is written.

Count: 1 e & a *etc.*

RHYTHM READING

Tap the following rhythm patterns using RH for notes with stems going up and LH for notes with stems going down. Tap hands separately first, and then hands together, always counting aloud.

🔊 4-27 (75)

1.

🔊 4-28 (76)

2.

🔊 4-29 (77)

3.

🔊 4-30 (78)

4.

Andante cantabile

from *Recreations for the Young*

🔊 4-31 (79)

Heinrich Enke (1811–1859)
Op. 6, No. 3

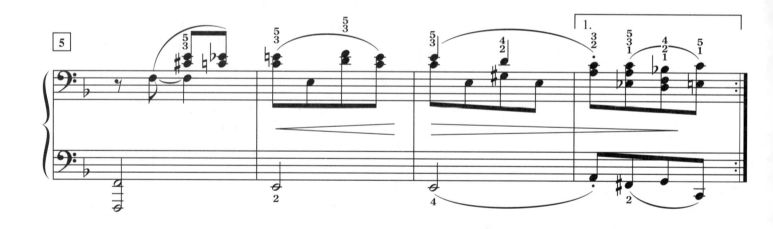

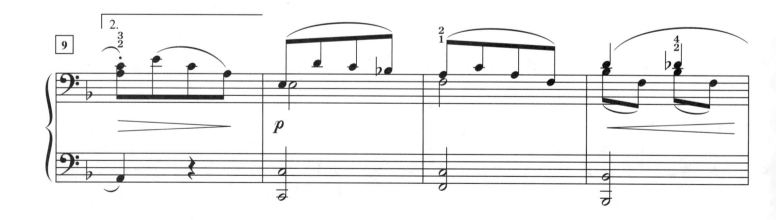

DUET: PRIMO

Student

Andante cantabile

from *Recreations for the Young*

Heinrich Enke (1811–1859)
Op. 6, No. 3

Andante cantabile (moving along in a singing style)
Both hands one octave higher than written throughout
espressivo (expressive)

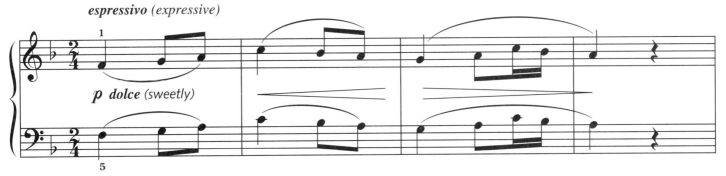

p dolce (sweetly)

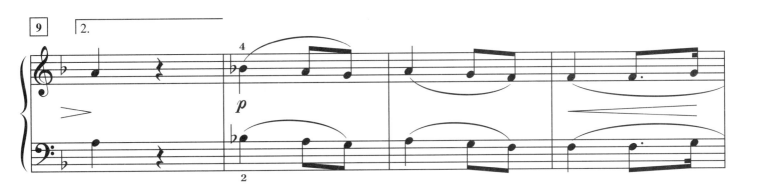

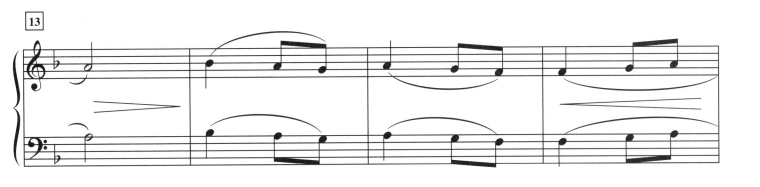

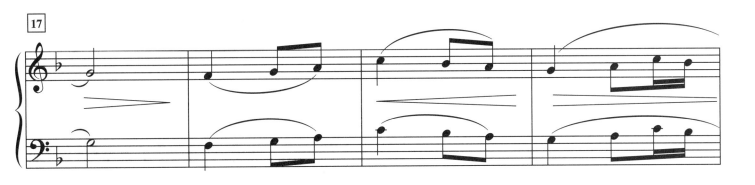

EAR TRAINING

Your teacher will clap a rhythm pattern.
Draw the missing notes in the box, using  or

🔊 **4-32 (80)**

a.

🔊 **4-33 (81)**

b.

🔊 **4-34 (82)**

c.

🔊 **4-35 (83)**

d.

Teacher: See page 146.

READING

Play the following example, counting aloud.

🔊 **4-36 (84)**

Slow march tempo

Seventh Chords

Objectives

Upon completion of this unit the student will be able to:

1. Play seventh chords on white keys.
2. Sight-read music that uses seventh chords.
3. Perform solo repertoire that uses seventh chords.
4. Aurally identify seventh chords.

Assignments

Week of _____

Write your assignments for the week in the space below.

_____

_____

_____

_____

_____

_____

_____

_____

_____

_____

_____

_____

_____

_____

Did You Know?

Franz Liszt

Franz Liszt (1811–1886), a Hungarian, exerted a major influence on music in the Romantic period both as a composer and a pianist. In addition to being a piano virtuoso, he was a conductor, critic, city music director and literary writer. He was the first composer to write a symphonic or tone poem, an orchestral piece based on a pictorial, literary or other non-musical idea. In addition to original works for piano, he transcribed music of other composers for the instrument, including the symphonies of Beethoven. During his lifetime, Liszt championed the music of Wagner. The modern piano recital was invented by Liszt. He was the first to place the piano on stage so that its lid reflected sound across the auditorium and so that the audience could see his profile as he performed. Liszt was a study in contradictions. He had intimate friends and at the same time was lonely; he was both religious and a womanizer; he was devoted to both Hungary and Paris. Unlike many composers, Liszt lived to age 75 and encouraged other artists throughout his life.

Seventh Chords

A seventh chord may be formed by adding to the root position triad a note that is a seventh above the root. Seventh chords in root position look like this:

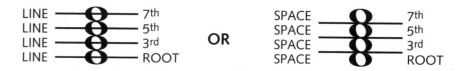

Playing Seventh Chords

Play the following seventh chord exercise hands separately.
Use fingers 5 3 2 1 for the LH.
Use fingers 1 2 3 5 for the RH and play one octave higher than written.

🔊 **4-37 (85)**

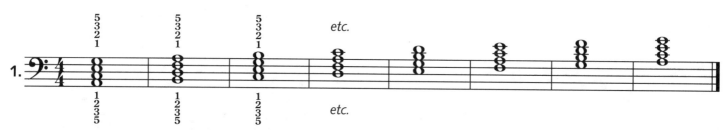

The 5th is sometimes omitted from the seventh chord. This makes it simple to play with one hand. Play the following exercise with the LH; then play with the RH, one octave higher than written.

🔊 **4-37 (85)**

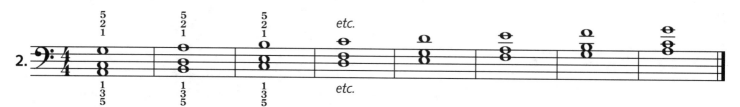

The 3rd is sometimes omitted from the seventh chord. This makes it simple to play with one hand. Play the following exercise with the LH; then play with the RH, one octave higher than written.

🔊 **4-37 (85)**

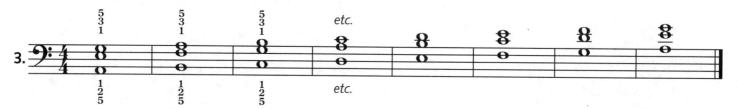

READING

Play the following examples, counting aloud.

🔊 4-38 (86)

Moderately slow

1.

🔊 4-39 (87)

Misterioso (mysteriously)

2.

St. Louis Blues

4-40 (88)

W. C. Handy (1873–1958)
arr. E. L. Lancaster

Slow blues tempo*

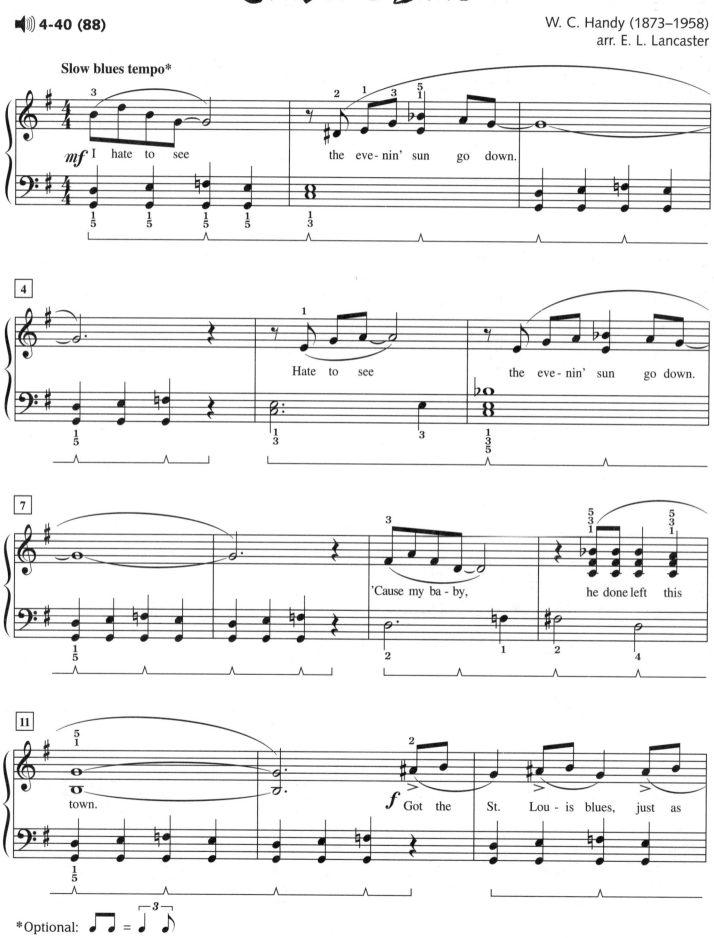

*Optional: ♪♪ = ♪ ♪ (3)

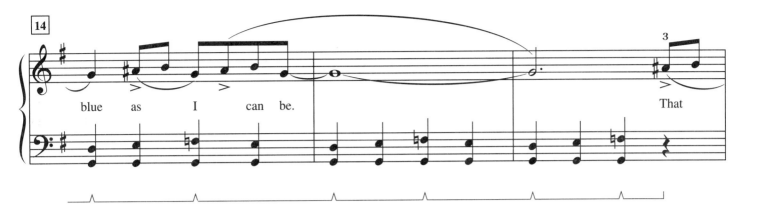

blue as I can be. That

man got a heart like a rock cast in the sea.

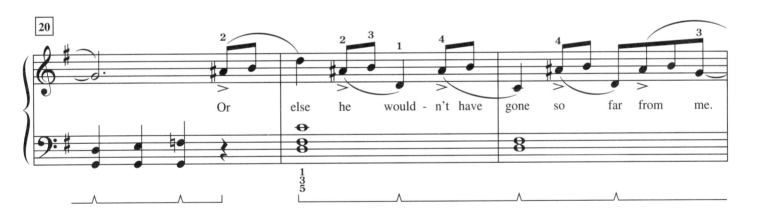

Or else he would - n't have gone so far from me.

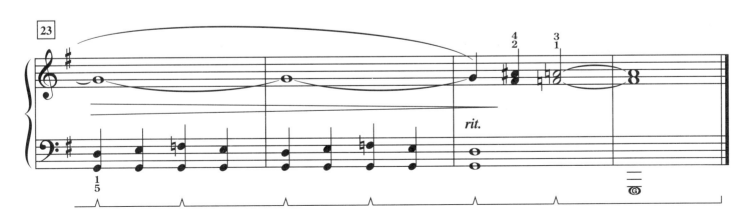

rit.

EAR TRAINING

1. Your teacher will play a major triad or a seventh chord.
   - Circle *major* if you hear a major triad.
   - Circle *seventh* if you hear a seventh chord.

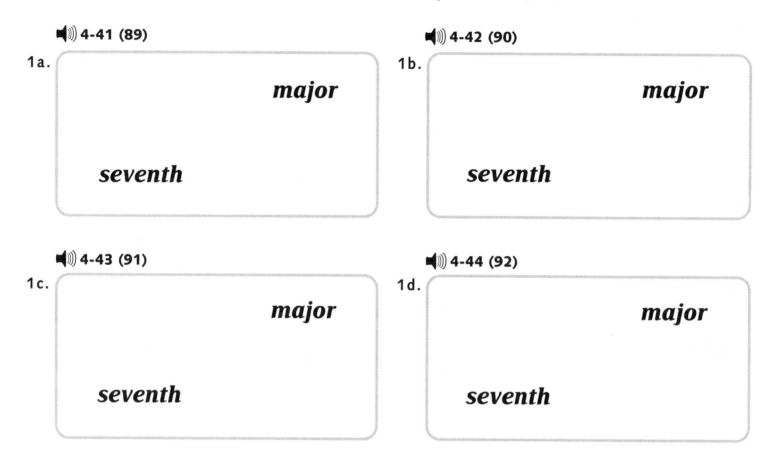

🔊 4-41 (89)

1a.

major

seventh

🔊 4-42 (90)

1b.

major

seventh

🔊 4-43 (91)

1c.

major

seventh

🔊 4-44 (92)

1d.

major

seventh

2. Your teacher will play a block seventh chord followed by a broken seventh chord. Write the notes of the broken chord in the order that they are played, using quarter notes.

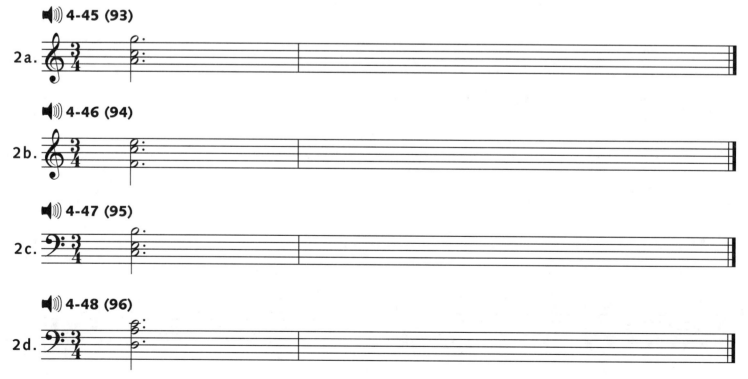

🔊 4-45 (93)

2a.

🔊 4-46 (94)

2b.

🔊 4-47 (95)

2c.

🔊 4-48 (96)

2d.

Teacher: See page 147.

Review Worksheet

Name _____   *Date* _____

1. Identify the scale below by writing its name on the indicated line. Write the correct RH fingering on the line above the staff and the correct LH fingering on the line below the staff.

 major

2. Identify the inversion of each chord in the indicated key by writing RP for root position, 1st for first inversion or 2nd for second inversion on the line below the staff.

3. Identify the quality of each chord by writing M for major, m for minor, A for augmented, or d for diminished on the line below the staff.

4. Identify each chord in the key of D major as I, IV or V7 by writing its name on the line.

5. Identify each chord in the key of D minor as i, iv or V7 by writing its name on the line.

Inversions of Seventh Chords

Objectives

Upon completion of this unit the student will be able to:

1. Play seventh chords and inversions on white keys.
2. Sight-read music that uses seventh chords and inversions.
3. Perform solo repertoire that uses seventh chords and inversions.
4. Harmonize a melody from a lead sheet that uses seventh chords and inversions.

Assignments

Week of _____

Write your assignments for the week in the space below.

_____

_____

_____

_____

_____

_____

_____

_____

_____

_____

_____

_____

_____

_____

Did You Know?

Sergei Rachmaninoff

Sergei Rachmaninoff (1873–1943) was born in Russia and studied at the Moscow Conservatory. He was famous as a composer, conductor and pianist. Even though he lived well into the 20th century, his music reflects the late romantic style of Russian composers such as Tchaikovsky. His keyboard music is full of rich and simple melodies combined with lush harmonies, reflecting the influence of the chants and church bells of the Russian Orthodox Church as well as his own passion and feelings. Rachmaninoff left Russia in 1917 and lived in Switzerland and the United States. He died in the United States shortly after he received his American citizenship. While he wrote works for other mediums, he is best known for his piano compositions including the Prelude in C-sharp Minor *and his piano concertos.*

Inversions of Seventh Chords

Four-note chords may be played in the following positions. All note names are the same in each position, but in a different order!

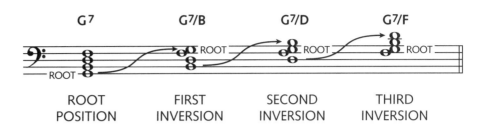

The first, second and third inversions are easily recognized by the interval of a 2nd in each chord. The top note of the 2nd is always the root!

Play the G7 chord and its inversions.

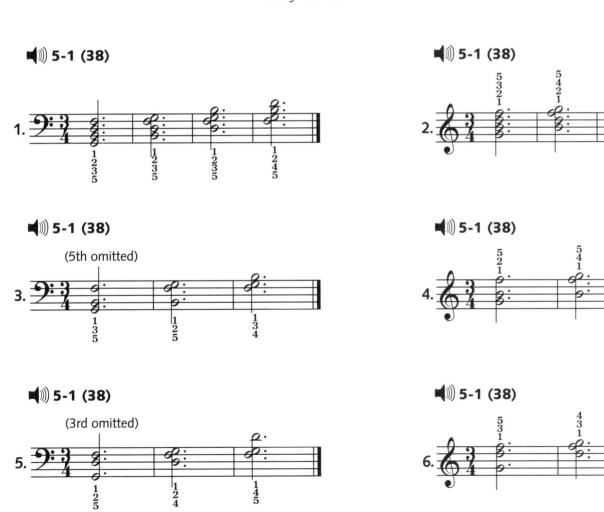

Sand Castles

5-2 (39)

Martha Mier

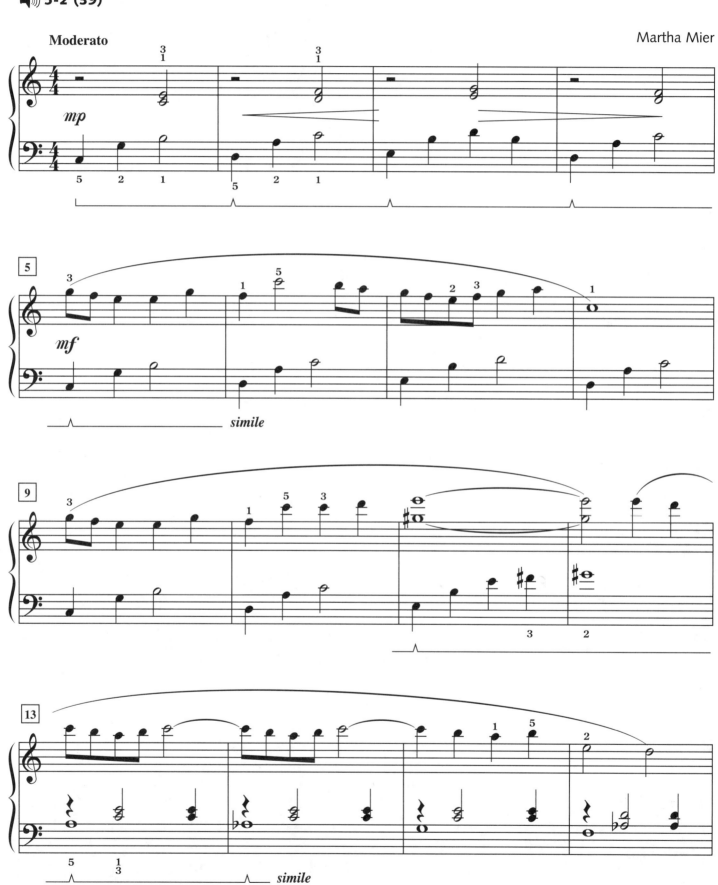

"Sand Castles" from ROMANTIC IMPRESSIONS, Book 1, by Martha Mier
Copyright © MCMXCIII by Alfred Publishing Co., Inc.

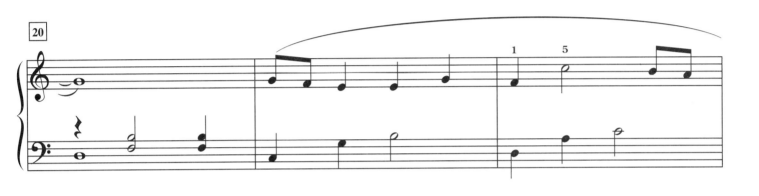

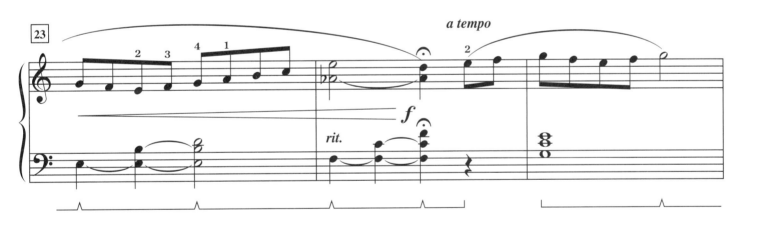

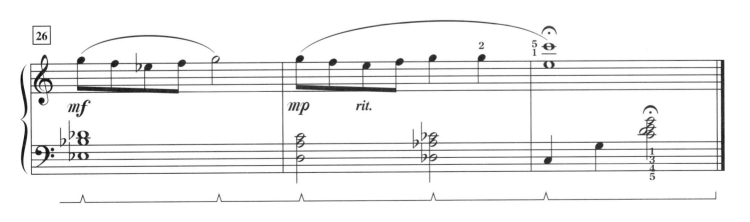

TECHNIQUE

READING

Play the following example, counting aloud.

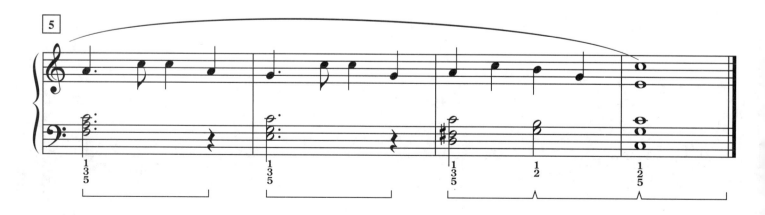

Harmonizing Melodies from a Lead Sheet

1. Using the indicated chords, harmonize the following melody by continuing the block-chord accompaniment pattern given in the first two measures.

Greensleeves

🔊 **5-7 (44)**

England

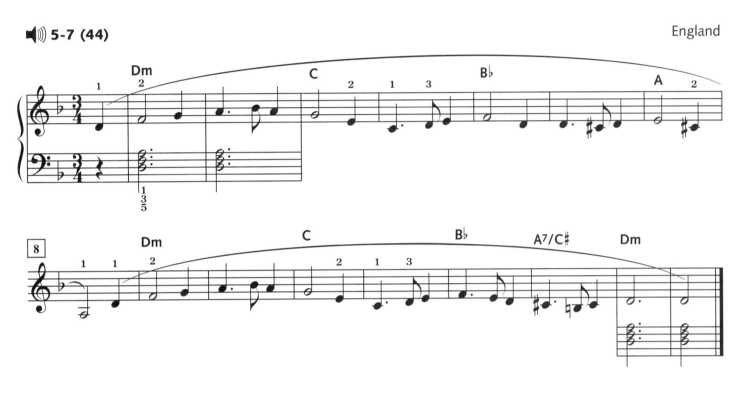

2. Using the indicated chords, harmonize the same melody by continuing the waltz-style accompaniment pattern given in the first two measures.

🔊 **5-8 (45)**

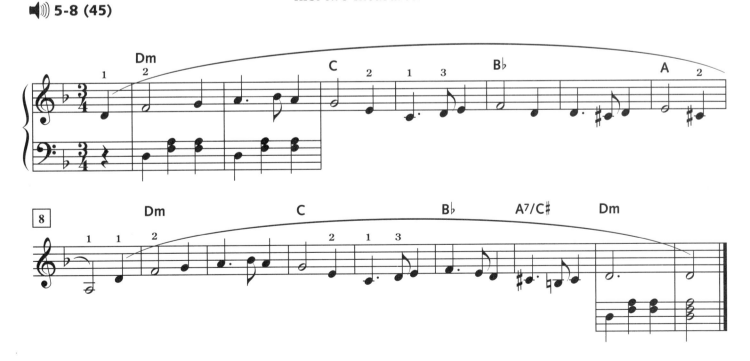

Syncopation and Ragtime

Objectives

Upon completion of this unit the student will be able to:

1. Tap two-part rhythm patterns.
2. Sight-read music that uses syncopation.
3. Aurally identify rhythm patterns that use syncopation.
4. Perform solo repertoire in ragtime style.

Assignments

Week of _____

Write your assignments for the week in the space below.

_____

_____

_____

_____

_____

_____

_____

_____

_____

_____

_____

_____

_____

_____

Did You Know?

Ragtime and Scott Joplin

Since ragtime first emerged in the 1890s, it has been one of the most-loved forms of piano music. Scott Joplin (1868–1917) is considered the foremost composer of ragtime; he became the leader of the style often associated with St. Louis, Missouri. In his day, Joplin's music, as well as that of other ragtime composers such as Joseph Lamb and James Scott, was widely published and sold many copies. Also adding to the popularity of this style was the abundance of piano rolls featuring the compositions of lesser-known composers. Ragtime's popularity began to wane after World War I when jazz music burst onto the scene. It wasn't until the early 1970s that ragtime enjoyed a resurgence in popularity. Once again, its energy, largely derived from the combination of a regular rhythmic bass in the left hand and a syncopated melody in the right hand, captured America's heart.

Syncopated Notes

Notes played between the main beats of a measure and held across the beat are called **syncopated** notes.

In the following rhythm, the first quarter note is syncopated:

Count: 1 & 2 & 3 & 4 &

READING

See how many syncopated notes you can find in this piece!

5-9 (46)

Song of the Mockingbird

Traditional

RHYTHM READING

Tap the following rhythm patterns using RH for notes with stems going up and LH for notes with stems going down. Tap hands separately first, and then hands together, always counting aloud.

5-10 (47)

5-11 (48)

5-12 (49)

5-13 (50)

READING

Play the following example, counting aloud.

🔊 **5-14 (51)**

Moderato

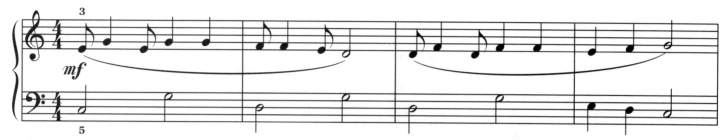

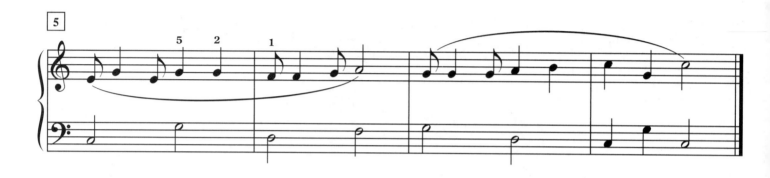

EAR TRAINING

Your teacher will clap a rhythm pattern.
Draw the missing notes in the third measure, using

🔊 **5-15 (52)**

a.

🔊 **5-16 (53)**

b.

🔊 **5-17 (54)**

c.

🔊 **5-18 (55)**

d.

Teacher: See page 147.

Ragtime Dance

5-19 (56)

Kenon D. Renfrow

Allegro moderato

*Note: Both hands read treble clef.

Key of B♭ Major

Objectives

Upon completion of this unit the student will be able to:

1. Play the B♭ major scale and arpeggio using traditional fingerings.
2. Build and play the primary chords in close position in the key of B♭ major.
3. Sight-read music that uses primary chords in the key of B♭ major.
4. Perform solo repertoire that uses primary chords in the key of B♭ major.
5. Aurally identify rhythm patterns and incorrect notes in the B♭ major scale.
6. Perform ensemble repertoire with partners.

Assignments

Week of _____

Write your assignments for the week in the space below.

_____

_____

_____

_____

_____

_____

_____

_____

_____

_____

Did You Know?

Claude Debussy

Claude Debussy and Maurice Ravel

Claude Debussy (1862–1918) and Maurice Ravel (1875–1937) were the leading French musicians at the turn of the century. Both are associated with Impressionism, a term borrowed from 19th century French painters and applied to music. Debussy was a master of tone color and invented ways of using chords that broke most conventional rules to produce exquisite harmonies. Debussy contributed to piano music in the 20th century through his two sets of Preludes in a similar manner that Chopin contributed to piano music in the 19th century. Even though Ravel was influenced by Debussy, his music is considered more dissonant and less emotional. In his music, one can find Spanish elements and jazz as well as references to children. One of his most popular pieces, Bolero, consists of two short themes of a single melody repeated over and over with different instrumental colors.

The B♭ Major Scale

Remember that the major scale is made up of two tetrachords joined by a whole step. The second tetrachord of the B♭ major scale begins on F.

There are two flats (B♭, E♭) in the B♭ major scale.

TECHNIQUE

🔊 **5-20 (57)**

1.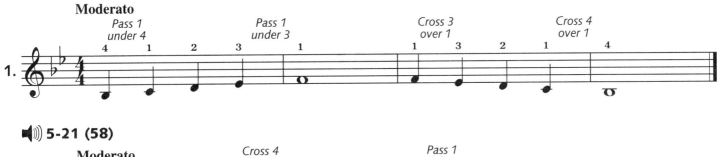

🔊 **5-21 (58)**

2.

Play the B♭ major scale hands separately.

🔊 **5-22 (59)**

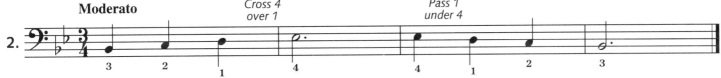

🔊 **5-22 (59)**

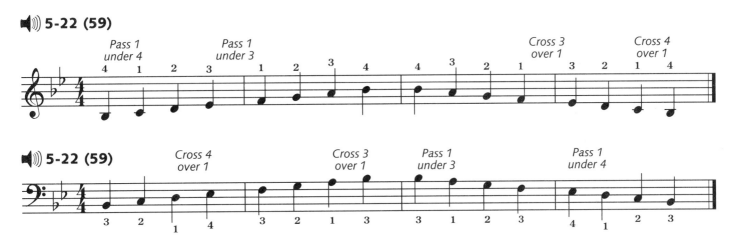

The B♭ Major Arpeggio

Play the B♭ major arpeggio hands separately.

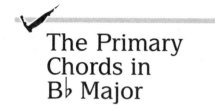

The Primary Chords in B♭ Major

Play the primary chords in B♭ major.

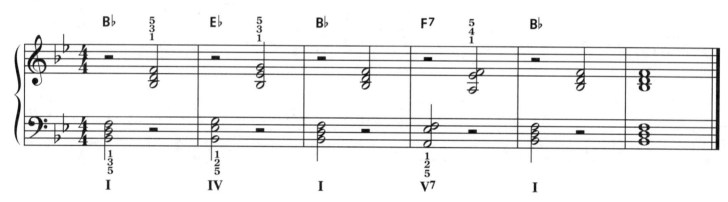

TECHNIQUE

READING

Play the following examples, counting aloud.

Theme from Bridal Chorus

from *Lohengrin*

Richard Wagner
(1813–1883)

🔊 5-26 (63)

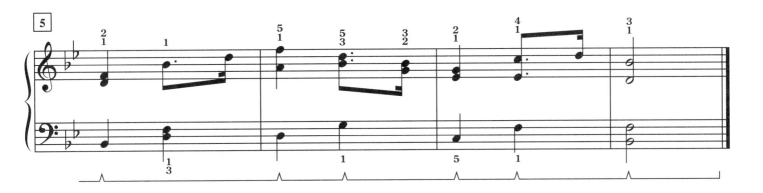

🔊 5-27 (64)

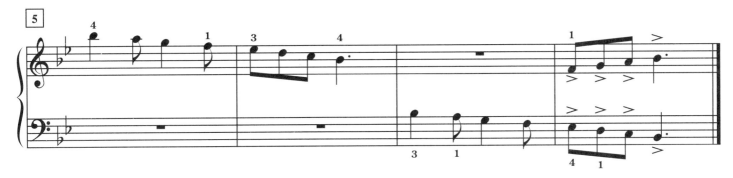

La Cucaracha

🔊 **5-28 (65)**

Traditional
arr. Kenon D. Renfrow

EAR TRAINING

1. Your teacher will play B♭ major scales. One note in each scale will be played incorrectly. Circle the incorrect note.

🔊 5-29 (66)

1a.

🔊 5-30 (67)

1b.

🔊 5-31 (68)

1c.

🔊 5-32 (69)

1d.

2. Your teacher will play B♭ major scales. Circle the rhythm pattern that you hear for each scale.

🔊 5-33 (70)

2a.

🔊 5-34 (71)

2b.

🔊 5-35 (72)

2c.

🔊 5-36 (73)

2d.

Teacher: See page 147.

In the Good Old Summer Time

5-37 (74)

George Evans
arr. E. L. Lancaster

Moderate waltz tempo

mf In the good old sum - mer time, In the good old sum - mer time,

Stroll - ing through the shad - y lanes with your ba - by mine; You

play RH one octave lower than written throughout

hold her hand and she holds yours, And that's a ver - y good sign   That

she's your toot - sey woot - sey   In the good old   sum - mer   time.

Key of G Minor

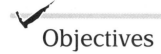

Objectives

Upon completion of this unit the student will be able to:

1. Play the G harmonic minor scale and arpeggio using traditional fingerings.
2. Build and play the primary chords in close position in the key of G minor.
3. Sight-read music that uses primary chords in the key of G minor.
4. Perform solo repertoire in the key of G minor.
5. Aurally distinguish i, iv and V7 chords in the key of G minor.
6. Harmonize a melody from a lead sheet, using triads and inversions.

Assignments

Week of _____

Write your assignments for the week in the space below.

_____

_____

_____

_____

_____

_____

_____

_____

Did You Know?

Jazz and Popular Music

*J*azz has its roots in the self-expression of the descendants of slaves, who created a music all their own. Even though jazz is the amalgamation of many different styles, it is the only major musical style that is truly American. Since jazz is improvisatory in nature, it has been handed down by oral tradition. This emphasis on improvisation is what has kept jazz fresh and has prompted its rapid, ever-changing development. Many types of jazz such as ragtime, blues, swing, bebop and fusion are still popular today despite their constant evolution.

The term popular music is often used to denote music that is enjoyed by those who have little or no knowledge of music theory. While jazz achieved great popularity in America during the first half of the 20th century, it never achieved the raging success of rock 'n' roll. Since Elvis Presley and the Beatles spawned the ideas for the pop, rock and country music of today, popular music continues to be the music of the masses.

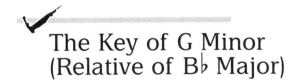

The Key of G Minor (Relative of B♭ Major)

G minor is the relative of B♭ major. Both keys have the same key signature (2 flats, B♭ & E♭).

Remember: The relative minor begins on the 6th tone of the major scale.

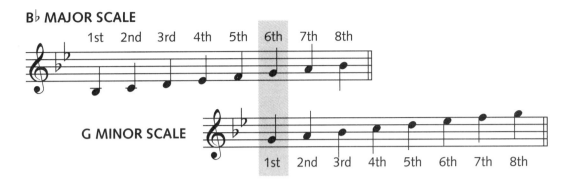

Play the G harmonic minor scale hands separately.

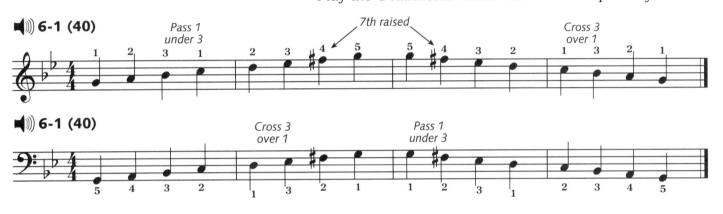

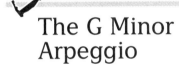

The G Minor Arpeggio

Play the G minor arpeggio hands separately.

The Primary Chords in G Minor

Play the primary chords in G minor.

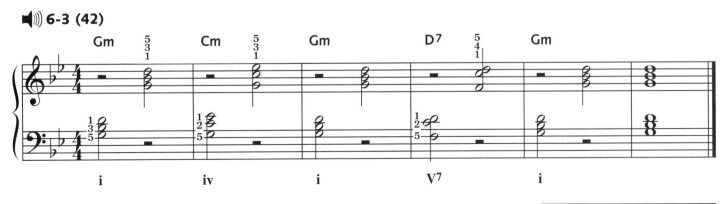

In the Hall of the Mountain King

from *Peer Gynt Suite*

 6-4 (43)

Edvard Grieg (1843–1907)
arr. E. L. Lancaster

March tempo

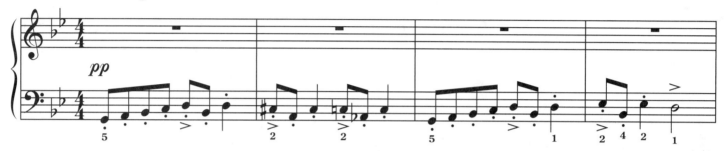

EAR TRAINING

1. Your teacher will play a left hand accompaniment pattern. Circle the pattern that you hear.

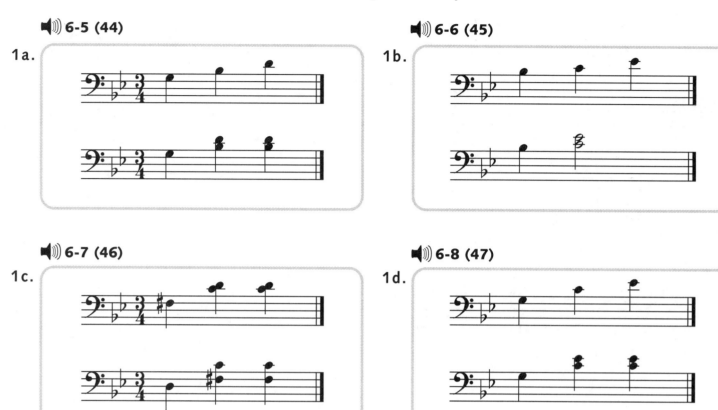

🔊 6-5 (44)

1a.

🔊 6-6 (45)

1b.

🔊 6-7 (46)

1c.

🔊 6-8 (47)

1d.

2. Your teacher will play a chord progression. Circle the progression that you hear.

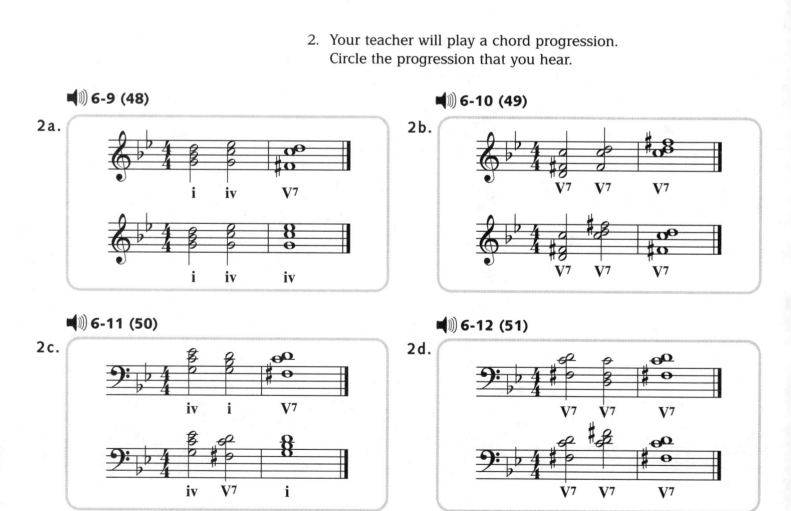

🔊 6-9 (48)

2a.

i   iv   V⁷

i   iv   iv

🔊 6-10 (49)

2b.

V⁷   V⁷   V⁷

V⁷   V⁷   V⁷

🔊 6-11 (50)

2c.

iv   i   V⁷

iv   V⁷   i

🔊 6-12 (51)

2d.

V⁷   V⁷   V⁷

V⁷   V⁷   V⁷

Teacher: See page 147.

READING

Play the following examples, counting aloud.

🔊 **6-13 (52)**

Allegro moderato

5

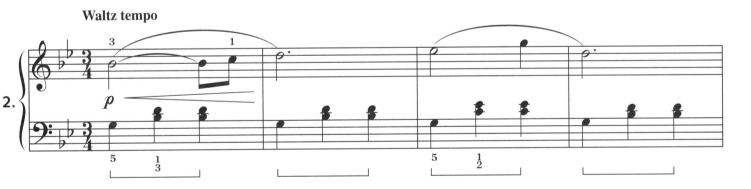

🔊 **6-14 (53)**

Waltz tempo

2.

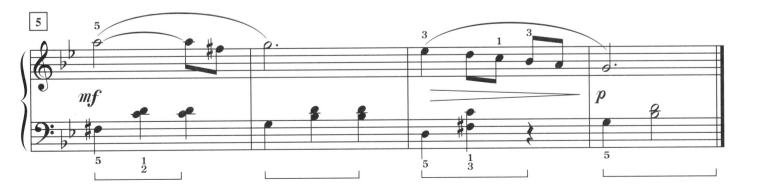

5

Harmonizing a Melody from a Lead Sheet

Using the indicated chords, harmonize the following melody by continuing the broken chord accompaniment pattern given in measure 1.

Scarborough Fair

6-15 (54)

England

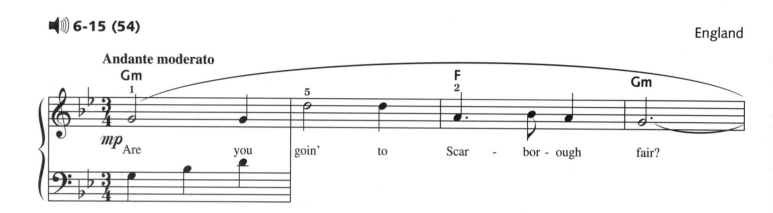

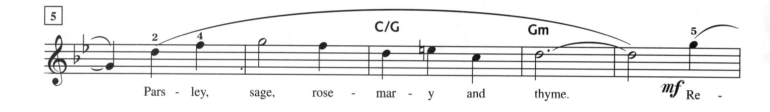

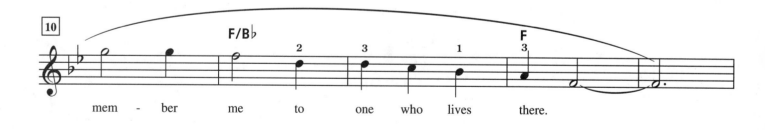

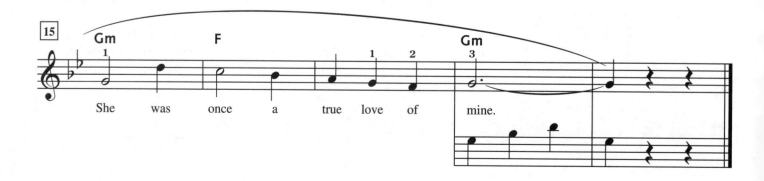

Review

Objectives

Upon completion of this unit the student will be able to:

1. Perform solo repertoire that uses syncopation.
2. Sight-read music in B♭ major and G minor.
3. Tap two-part rhythm patterns
4. Aurally distinguish I, IV and V7 chords in the key of B♭ major.

Assignments

Week of _____

Write your assignments for the week in the space below.

_____

_____

_____

_____

_____

_____

_____

_____

_____

_____

_____

_____

_____

_____

Did You Know?

Music Technology

Even though inventors began to develop electric musical instruments well before 1900, it wasn't until Robert Moog (1934–) invented the first music synthesizer in 1964 that these instruments began to be used in the performance of popular music. With the rapid development in electronic technology, manufacturers developed instruments with more capabilities, lower prices, and more portability than their early ancestors. With the advent of the musical instrument digital interface (MIDI) all of the major manufacturers agreed to make their instruments compatible so that sharing information is easier. Today, digital pianos, electronic keyboards and computers are used extensively in music teaching and performing.

Just Struttin' Along

🔊 **6-16 (55)**

Martha Mier

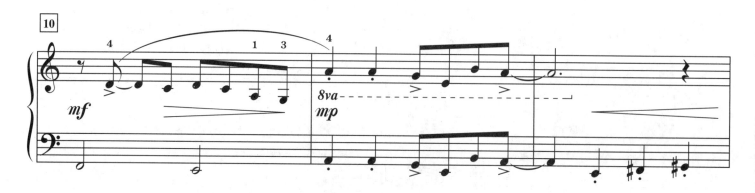

"Just Struttin' Along" from JAZZ, RAGS 'N' BLUES, Book 1, by Martha Mier
Copyright © MCMXCIII by Alfred Publishing Co., Inc.

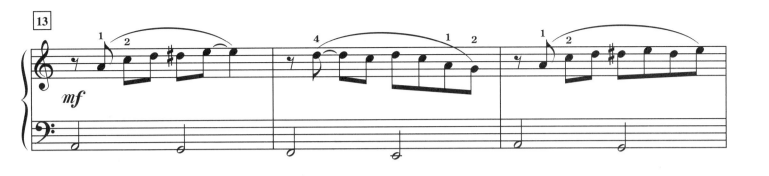

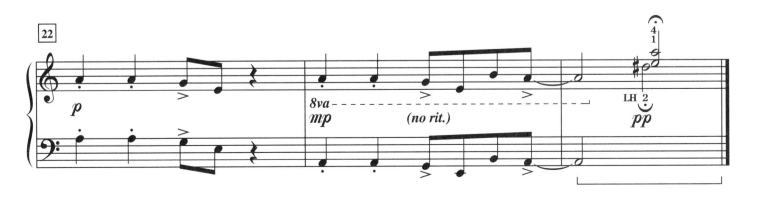

READING

Play the following examples, counting aloud.

🔊 **6-17 (56)**

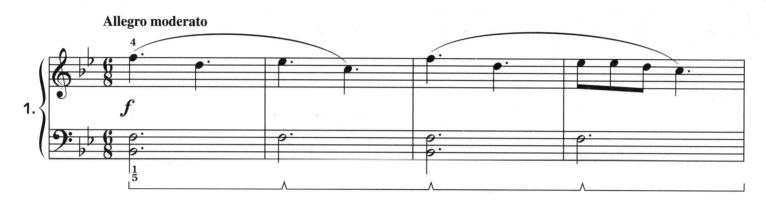

1.

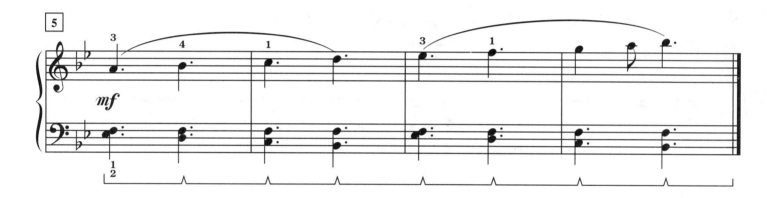

5

🔊 **6-18 (57)**

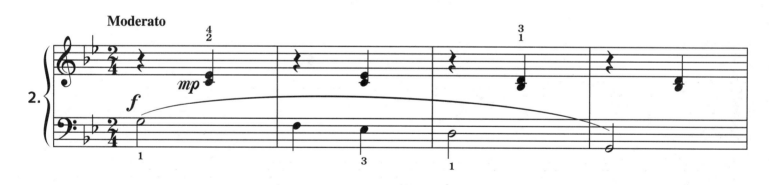

2.

5

RHYTHM READING

Tap the following rhythm patterns using RH for notes with stems going up and LH for notes with stems going down. Tap hands separately first, and then hands together, always counting aloud.

🔊 6-19 (58)

🔊 6-20 (59)

🔊 6-21 (60)

🔊 6-22 (61)

EAR TRAINING

Your teacher will play a block chord followed by a broken chord. Write the notes of the broken chord in the order that they are played, using quarter notes.

🔊 6-23 (62)

🔊 6-24 (63)

🔊 6-25 (64)

🔊 6-26 (65)

Teacher: See page 147.

Review Worksheet

Name _____   Date _____

1. Identify each scale below by writing its name on the indicated line. Write the correct RH fingering
    on the line above the staff and the correct LH fingering on the line below the staff.

_____ major

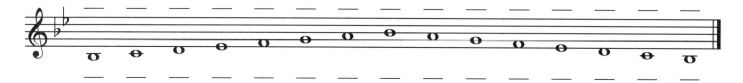

_____ minor

2. Identify the inversion of each seventh chord in the indicated key by writing
    RP for root position or 1st for first inversion on the line below the staff.

3. Identify each chord in the key of B♭ major as I, IV or V7 by writing its name on the line.

4. Identify each chord in the key of G minor as i, iv or V7 by writing its name on the line.

Burleske

6-27 (66)

Leopold Mozart
(1719–1787)

Rondino

Jean-Philippe Rameau
(1683–1764)

Ragtime Rondino

(Based on Jean-Phillipe Rameau's *Rondino*)

🔊 **6-29 (68)**

Kenon D. Renfrow

Hava Nagila

Traditional
arr. Kenon D. Renfrow

Silent Night

🔊 6-31 (70)

Franz Grüber (1787–1863)
arr. Gayle Kowalchyk & E. L. Lancaster

Gently, moderately slow

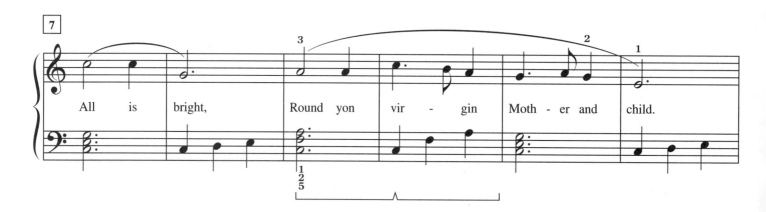

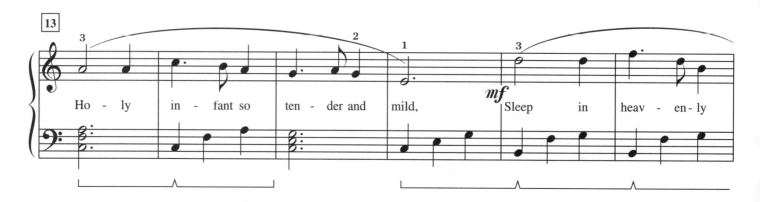

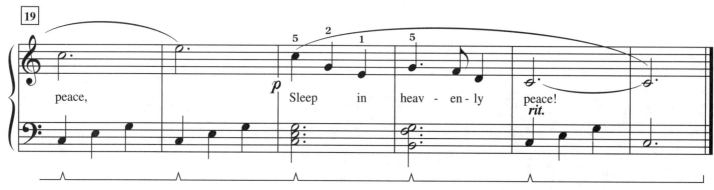

Piano Concerto No. 2

Theme from the 3rd Movement

Sergei Rachmaninoff (1873–1943)
Op.18
arr. Kenon D. Renfrow

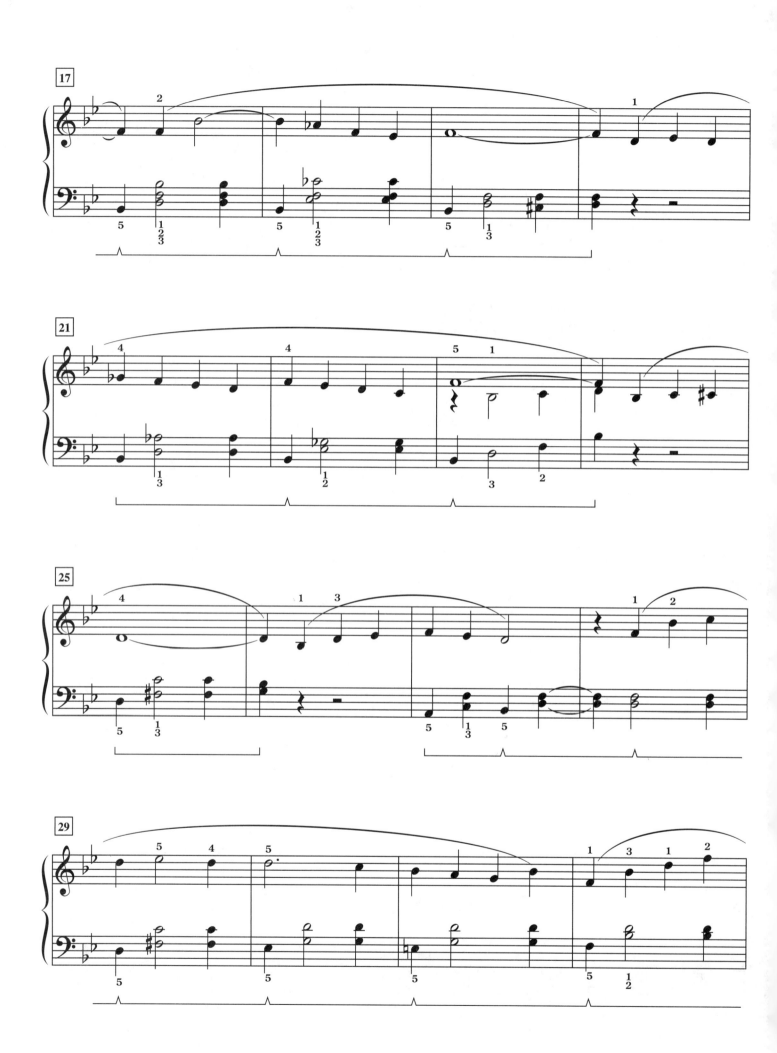

A Pleasant Morning

6-33 (72)

Jean Louis Streabbog (1835–1886)
Op. 63, No. 1

Allegro moderato

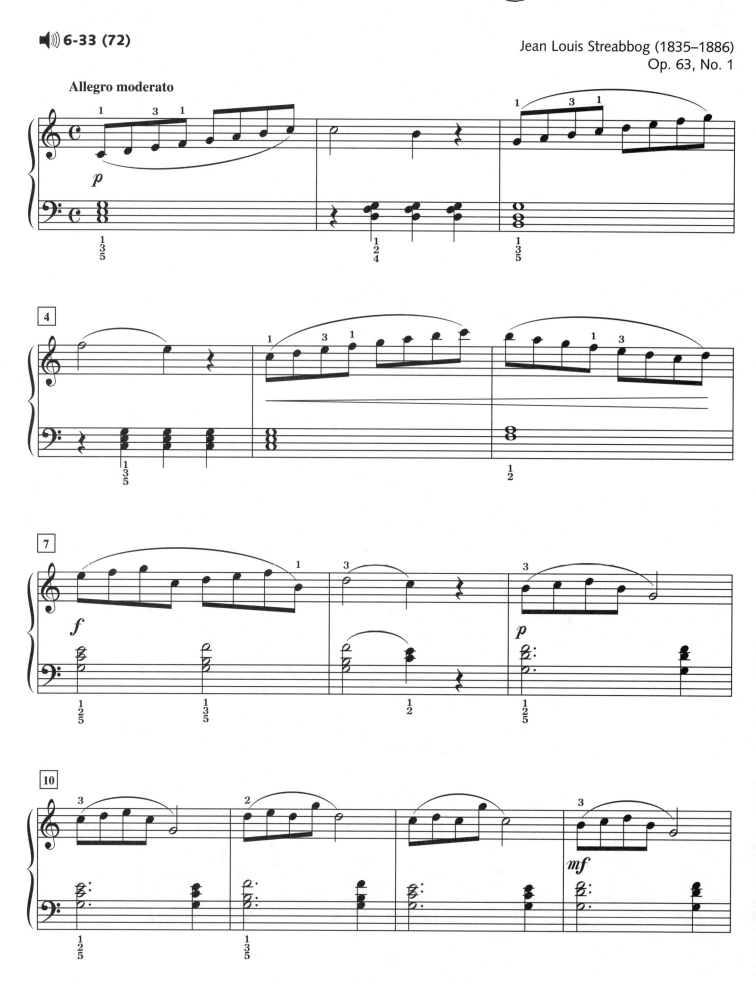

Menuet in G Major

from the *Notebook for Anna Magdalena*

6-34 (73)

Johann Sebastian Bach
(1685–1750)

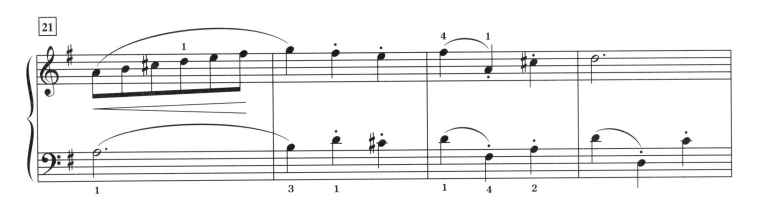

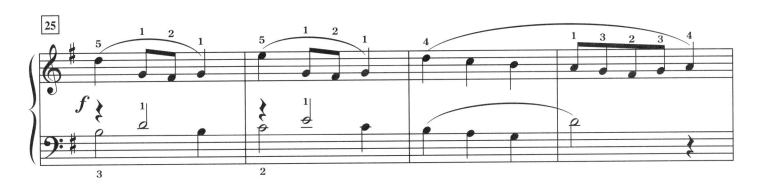

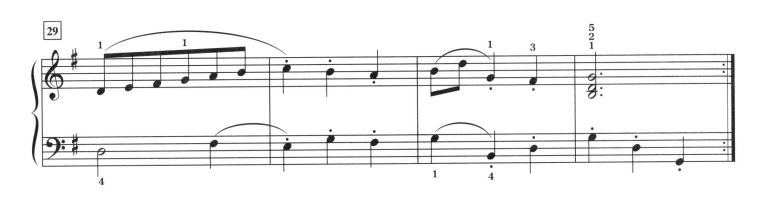

Liebestraum

Theme from No. 3

🔊 6-35 (74)

Franz Liszt (1811–1886)
arr. Kenon D. Renfrow

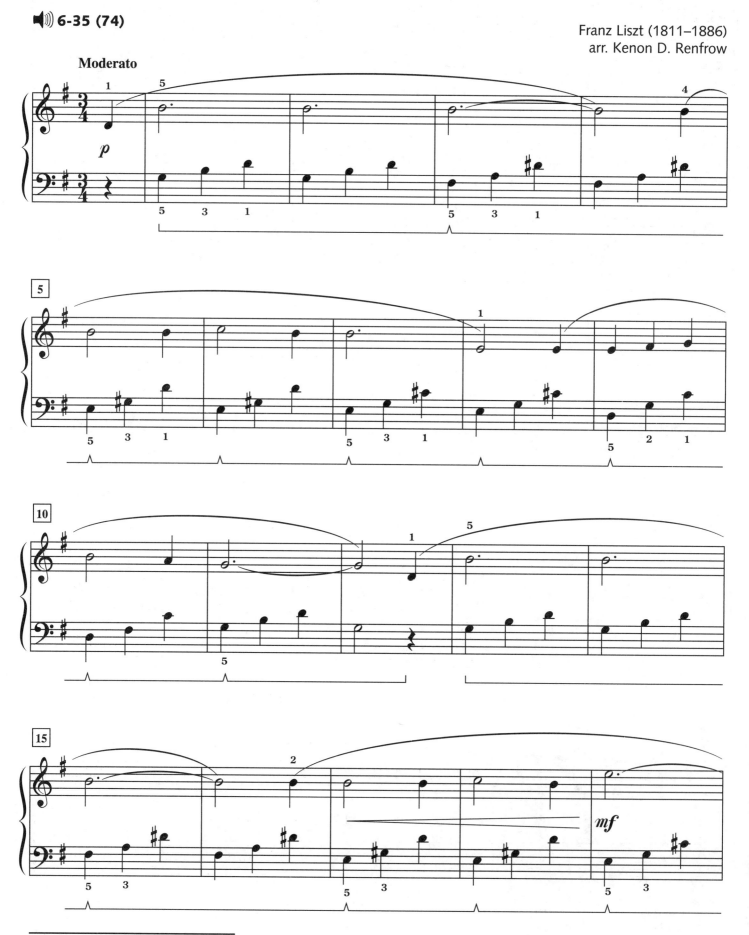

Sonatina in C Major

First Movement

Frank Lynes (1858–1913)
Op. 39, No. 1

The Entertainer

🔊 **6-37 (76)**

Scott Joplin (1868–1917)
arr. E. L. Lancaster &
Kenon D. Renfrow

Not fast!

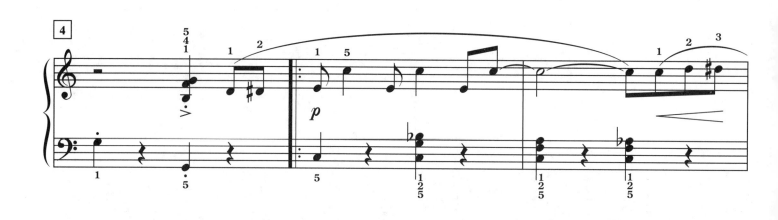

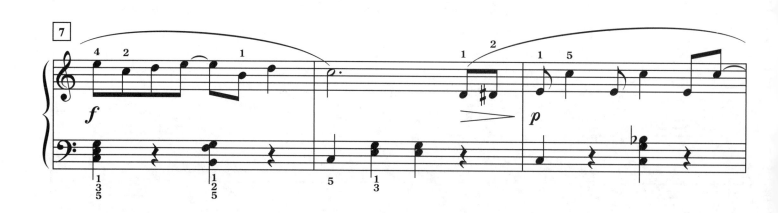

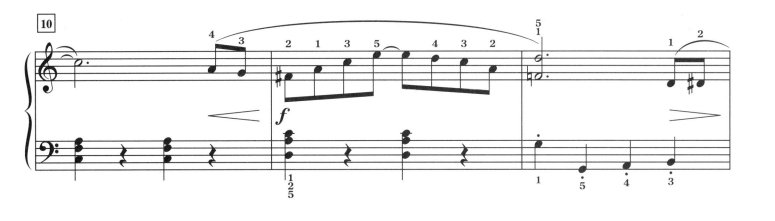

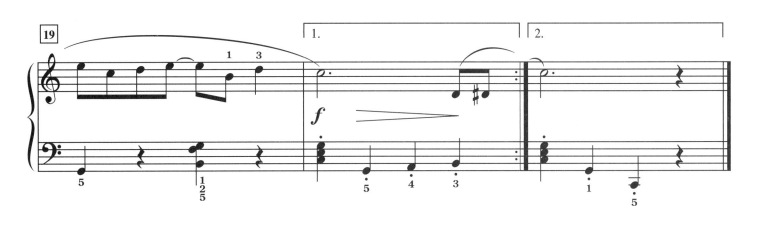

Prelude in C Major

from *The Well-Tempered Clavier, Book 1*

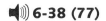 **6-38 (77)**

Johann Sebastian Bach
(1685–1750)

Andante con moto

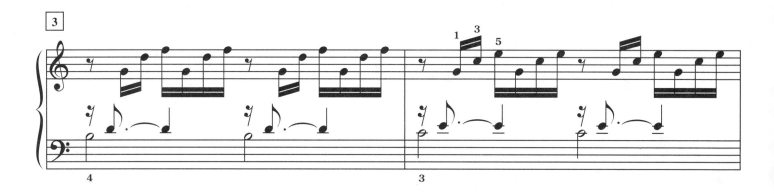

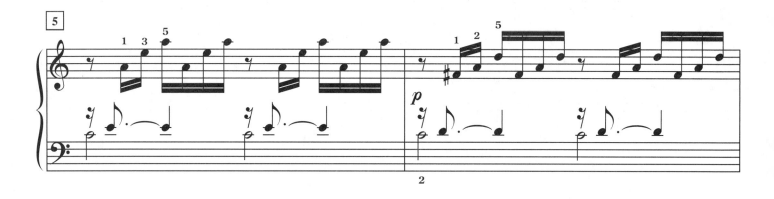

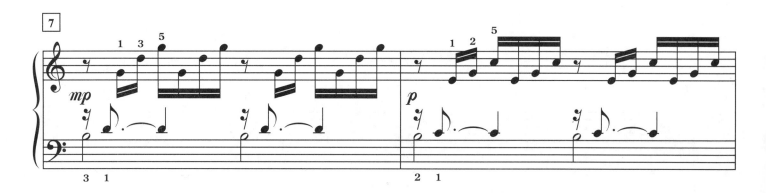

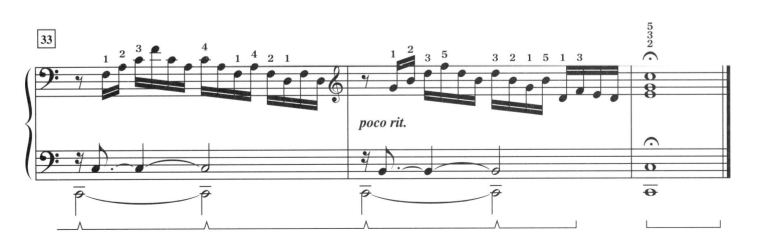

Spinning Song

Albert Ellmenreich (1816–1905)
Op. 14, No. 4

6-39 (78)

Appendix A

TEACHER'S EXAMPLES (EAR TRAINING)

Page 15 (Play)

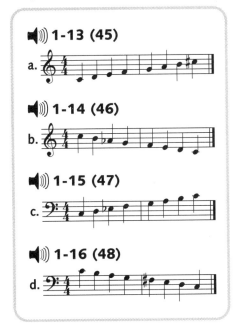

Page 20 (Play)

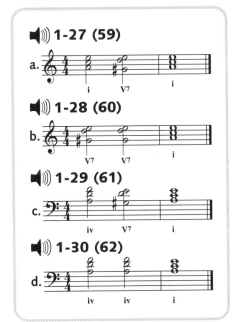

Page 24 (Play)

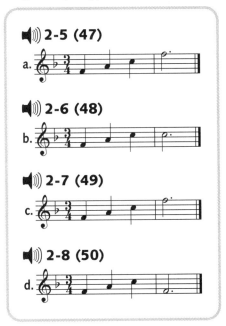

Page 27 (Play)

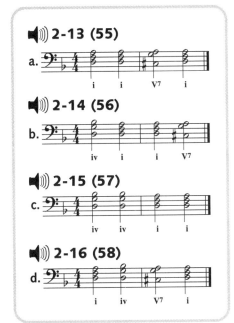

Page 35 (Clap)

Page 43 (Play)

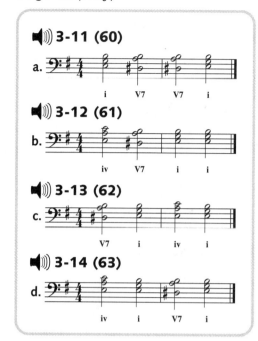

3-11 (60)
a. i V7 V7 i

3-12 (61)
b. iv V7 i i

3-13 (62)
c. V7 i iv i

3-14 (63)
d. iv i V7 i

Page 52 (Play)

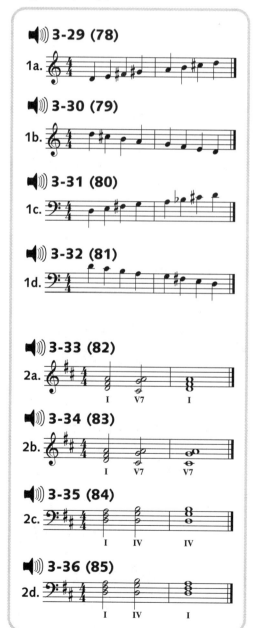

3-29 (78)
1a.

3-30 (79)
1b.

3-31 (80)
1c.

3-32 (81)
1d.

3-33 (82)
2a. I V7 I

3-34 (83)
2b. I V7 V7

3-35 (84)
2c. I IV IV

3-36 (85)
2d. I IV I

Page 70 (Clap)

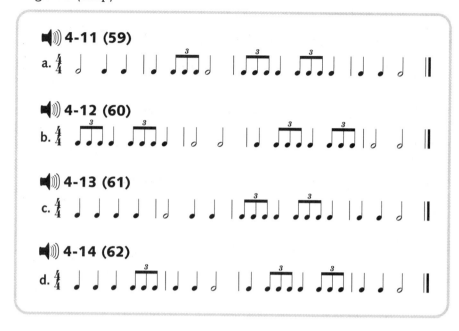

4-11 (59)
a.

4-12 (60)
b.

4-13 (61)
c.

4-14 (62)
d.

Page 74 (Clap)

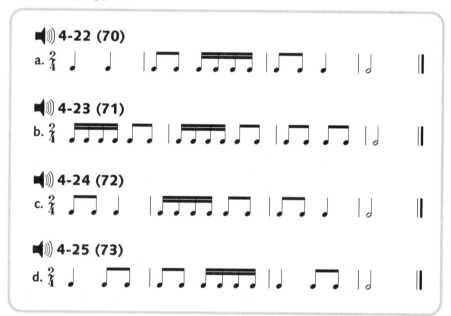

4-22 (70)
a.

4-23 (71)
b.

4-24 (72)
c.

4-25 (73)
d.

Page 80 (Clap)

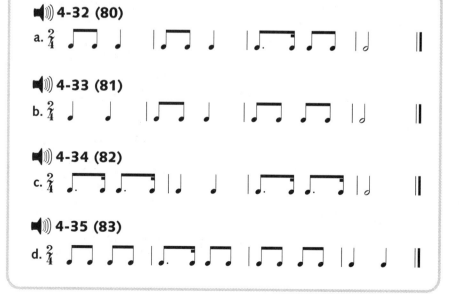

4-32 (80)
a.

4-33 (81)
b.

4-34 (82)
c.

4-35 (83)
d.

Page 86 (Play)

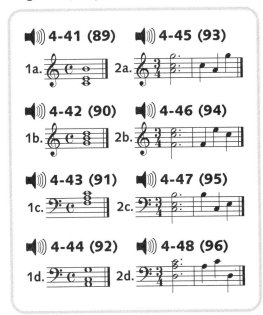

Page 96 (Clap)

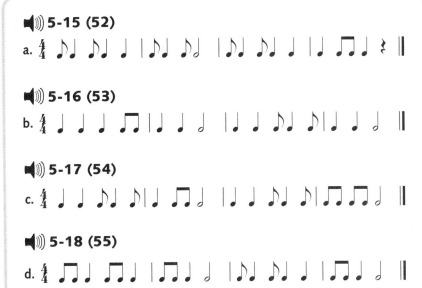

Page 103 (Play)

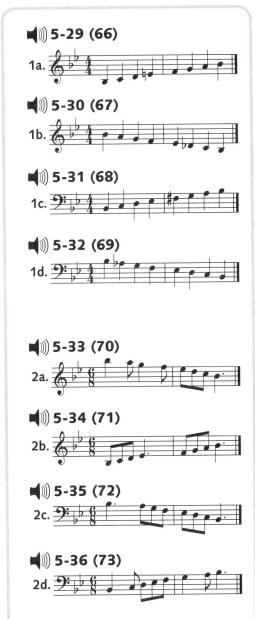

Page 110 (Play)

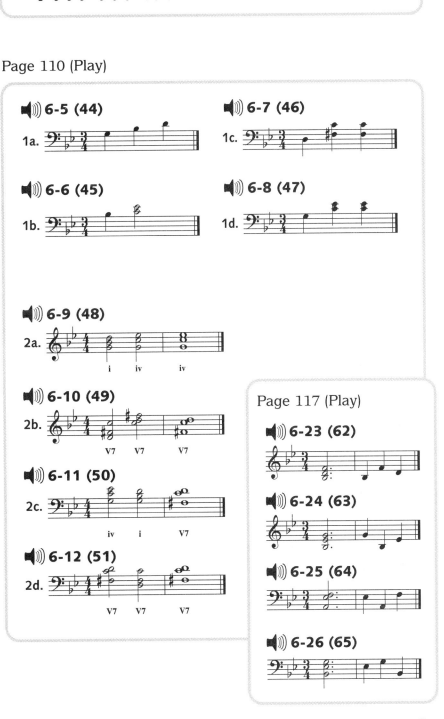

Appendix B

Note: A dot (•) above a fingering indicates a black key.

Major Scales

Key		Fingering		Key		Fingering	
C	RH:	1 2 3 1 2 3 4	1 2 3 1 2 3 4 5	G♭ (F♯)	RH:	•2 •3 •4 1 •2 •3 1	•2 •3 •4 1 •2 •3 1 •2
	LH:	5 4 3 2 1 3 2	1 4 3 2 1 3 2 1		LH:	4 3 2 1 3 2 1	4 3 2 1 3 2 1 4
G	RH:	1 2 3 1 2 3 •4	1 2 3 1 2 3 •4 5	D♭ (C♯)	RH:	•2 3 1 •2 •3 4 1	•2 3 1 •2 •3 4 1 •2
	LH:	5 4 3 2 1 3 2	1 4 3 2 1 3 2 1		LH:	3 2 1 4 3 2 1	3 2 1 4 3 2 1 3
D	RH:	1 2 •3 1 2 3 •4	1 2 •3 1 2 3 •4 5	A♭	RH:	•3 •4 1 •2 3 1 2	•3 •4 1 •2 3 1 2 •3
	LH:	5 4 3 2 1 3 2	1 4 3 2 1 3 2 1		LH:	3 2 1 4 3 2 1	3 2 1 4 3 2 1 3
A	RH:	1 2 •3 1 2 •3 •4	1 2 •3 1 2 •3 •4 5	E♭	RH:	•3 1 •2 •3 4 1 2	•3 1 •2 •3 4 1 2 •3
	LH:	5 4 3 2 1 3 2	1 4 3 2 1 3 2 1		LH:	3 2 1 4 3 2 1	3 2 1 4 3 2 1 3
E	RH:	1 •2 •3 1 •2 •3 •4	1 •2 •3 1 •2 •3 •4 5	B♭	RH:	•4 1 •2 3 1 2 3	•4 1 •2 3 1 2 3 •4
	LH:	5 4 3 2 1 3 2	1 4 3 2 1 3 2 1		LH:	3 2 1 4 3 2 1	3 2 1 4 3 2 1 3
B	RH:	1 •2 •3 1 •2 •3 •4	1 •2 •3 1 •2 •3 •4 5	F	RH:	1 2 3 •4 1 2 3	1 2 3 •4 1 2 3 4
	LH:	4 3 2 1 4 3 2	1 3 2 1 4 3 2 1		LH:	5 4 3 2 1 3 2	1 4 3 2 1 3 2 1

Major Arpeggios

Key		Fingering		Key		Fingering	
C	RH:	1 2 3	1 2 3 5	G♭ (F♯)	RH:	•1 •2 •3	•1 2 3 •5
	LH:	5 4 2	1 4 2 1		LH:	5 3 2	1 3 2 1
G	RH:	1 2 3	1 2 3 5	D♭ (C♯)	RH:	•4 1 •2	•4 1 •2 •4
	LH:	5 4 2	1 4 2 1		LH:	2 1 4	2 1 4 2
D	RH:	1 •2 3	1 •2 3 5	A♭	RH:	•4 1 •2	•4 1 •2 •4
	LH:	5 3 2	1 3 2 1		LH:	2 1 4	2 1 4 2
A	RH:	1 •2 3	1 •2 3 5	E♭	RH:	•4 1 •2	•4 1 2 •4
	LH:	5 3 2	1 3 2 1		LH:	2 1 4	2 1 4 2
E	RH:	1 •2 3	1 •2 3 5	B♭	RH:	•4 1 2	•4 1 2 •4
	LH:	5 3 2	1 3 2 1		LH:	3 2 1	3 2 1 3
B	RH:	1 •2 •3	1 •2 •3 5	F	RH:	1 2 3	1 2 3 5
	LH:	5 3 2	1 3 2 1		LH:	5 4 2	1 4 2 1

Harmonic Minor Scales

Key		Fingering	
a	RH:	1 2 3 1 2 3 4̇	1 2 3 1 2 3 4̇ 5
	LH:	5 4 3 2 1 3 2	1 4 3 2 1 3 2 1
e	RH:	1 2̇ 3 1 2 3 4̇	1 2̇ 3 1 2 3 4̇ 5
	LH:	5 4 3 2 1 3 2	1 4 3 2 1 3 2 1
b	RH:	1 2̇ 3 1 2̇ 3 4	1 2̇ 3 1 2 3 4̇ 5
	LH:	4 3 2 1 4 3 2	1 3 2 1 4 3 2 1
f#	RH:	3̇ 4̇ 1 2 3 1 2	3̇ 4̇ 1 2 3 1 2 3̇
	LH:	4 3 2 1 3 2 1	4 3 2 1 3 2 1 4
c#	RH:	3̇ 4̇ 1 2̇ 3 1 2	3̇ 4̇ 1 2̇ 3 1 2 3̇
	LH:	3 2 1 4 3 2 1	3 2 1 4 3 2 1 3
g# (ab)	RH:	3̇ 4̇ 1 2̇ 3 1 2	3̇ 4̇ 1 2̇ 3 1 2 3̇
	LH:	3 2 1 4 3 2 1	3 2 1 4 3 2 1 3
eb (d#)	RH:	3̇ 1 2̇ 3̇ 4 1 2	3̇ 1 2̇ 3̇ 4 1 2 3̇
	LH:	2 1 4 3 2 1 3	2 1 4 3 2 1 3 2
bb (a#)	RH:	4̇ 1 2̇ 3 1 2 3	4̇ 1 2̇ 3 1 2 3 4̇
	LH:	2 1 3 2 1 4 3	2 1 3 2 1 4 3 2
f	RH:	1 2 3 4̇ 1 2 3	1 2 3̇ 4̇ 1 2̇ 3 4
	LH:	5 4 3 2 1 3 2	1 4 3 2 1 3 2 1
c	RH:	1 2 3 1 2 3 4̇	1 2̇ 3 1 2 3 4 5
	LH:	5 4 3 2 1 3 2	1 4 3 2 1 3 2 1
g	RH:	1 2 3 1 2 3 4̇	1 2̇ 3 1 2̇ 3 4̇ 5
	LH:	5 4 3 2 1 3 2	1 4 3 2 1 3 2 1
d	RH:	1 2 3 1 2̇ 3 4̇	1 2 3 1 2 3 4̇ 5
	LH:	5 4 3 2 1 3 2	1 4 3 2 1 3 2 1

Minor Arpeggios

Key		Fingering	
a	RH:	1 2 3	1 2 3 5
	LH:	5 4 2	1 4 2 1
e	RH:	1 2 3	1 2 3 5
	LH:	5 4 2	1 4 2 1
b	RH:	1 2 3̇	1 2 3̇ 5
	LH:	5 4 2	1 4 2 1
f#	RH:	4̇ 1 2̇	4̇ 1 2̇ 4̇
	LH:	2 1 4	2 1 4 2
c#	RH:	4̇ 1 2	4̇ 1 2̇ 4̇
	LH:	2 1 4	2 1 4 2
g# (ab)	RH:	4̇ 1 2̇	4̇ 1 2̇ 4̇
	LH:	2 1 4	2 1 4 2
eb (d#)	RH:	1̇ 2̇ 3̇	1̇ 2̇ 3̇ 5̇
	LH:	5 4 2	1 4 2 1
bb (a#)	RH:	2̇ 3 1	2̇ 3 1 2̇
	LH:	3 2 1	3 2 1 3
f	RH:	1 2̇ 3	1 2̇ 3 5
	LH:	5 4 2	1 4 2 1
c	RH:	1 2̇ 3	1 2̇ 3 5
	LH:	5 4 2	1 4 2 1
g	RH:	1 2̇ 3	1 2̇ 3 5
	LH:	5 4 2	1 4 2 1
d	RH:	1 2 3	1 2 3 5
	LH:	5 4 2	1 4 2 1

Appendix C

Accelerando . . . . gradually faster.

Accent sign (>) . . . . . . placed over or under a note that gets special emphasis; play that note louder.

Adagio . . . . slowly.

Alla breve (¢) . . . . cut time or $\frac{2}{2}$ time.

Allegretto . . . . moderately fast.

Allegro . . . . quickly, happily.

Andante . . . . moving along (the word actually means "walking").

Arpeggio . . . . broken chord; pitches are sounded successively rather than simultaneously.

A tempo . . . . resume original speed.

Binary form (AB) . . . . a piece divided into two sections: A and B.

Cantabile . . . . in a singing style.

Chromatic scale . . . . . made up entirely of half steps; it goes up and down, using every key, black and white.

Coda . . . . an added ending.

Coda sign (⊕) . . . . indication to proceed to coda.

Common time (C) . . . same as $\frac{4}{4}$ time.

Crescendo (<) . . . . . gradually louder.

Cut time (¢) . . . . same as $\frac{2}{2}$ time; alla breve.

D. C. al Coda . . . . repeat from the beginning to ⊕, then skip to Coda.

D. C. al Fine . . . . repeat from the beginning to the word "Fine."

Decrescendo (>) . . . gradually softer.

Diminuendo (>) . . . . gradually softer.

Dolce . . . . sweetly.

Espressivo . . . . expressive.

Fermata (⌒) . . . . hold the note under the sign longer than its full value.

Fine . . . . the end.

First ending (1.⎯) . play first time only.

Flat sign (♭) . . . . lowers a note one half step; play the next key to the left, whether black or white.

Forte (f) . . . . loud.

Fortissimo (ff) . . . . . very loud.

Grand staff . . . . the bass staff and the treble staff joined together by a brace.

Half step . . . . the distance from any key to the very next key above or below it (black or white—there is no key between).

Harmonic intervals . . distances between notes or keys that are played together.

Incomplete measure . . a measure at the beginning of a piece with fewer counts than indicated in the time signature. The missing beats are usually found in the last measure.

Intervals . . . . distances between notes or keys.

Key signature . . . . the number of sharps or flats in any key, written at the beginning of each line.

Largo . . . . very slow.

Legato . . . . smoothly connected.

Leger line . . . . used above or below the staff to extend its range.

Leggiero . . . . lightly.

Maestoso . . . . majestically.

Melodic intervals . . . . distance between notes or keys that are played separately.

Mezzo forte (mf) . . . . . moderately loud.

Mezzo piano (mp) . . . . moderately soft.

Misterioso . . . . mysteriously.

Moderato . . . . moderately.

Molto . . . . much.

Moto . . . . motion.

Natural sign (♮) . . . . . cancels a sharp or flat.

Octave . . . . the distance from one key on the keyboard to the next key (lower or higher) with the same letter name.

Octave sign (*8va*) . . . . play eight scale tones (one octave) higher when the sign is above the notes; eight scale tones lower when the sign is below the notes.

Pedal mark (⎿⎽⎺⏌) . . press the damper, hold it, and release it.

Phrase . . . . musical thought or sentence.

Pianissimo (pp) . . . . . very soft.

Piano (p) . . . . soft.

Poco . . . . little.

Poco moto . . . . a little motion.

Repeat sign (:‖) . . . . . repeat from the beginning, or from the first repeat (‖:).

Rests . . . . signs for silence.

Ritardando
(*rit.* or *ritard.*) . . . . gradually slowing.

Second ending (2.⎯) . play second time only.

Sharp sign (♯) . . . . raises a note one half step; play the next key to the right, whether black or white.

Simile . . . . in the same manner.

Slur . . . . curved line over or under notes on different lines or spaces. Slurs mean to play legato.

Staccato . . . . dots over or under notes meaning to play short, detached.

Subito (*sub.*) . . . . suddenly.

Syncopated notes . . . . notes played between the main beats of a measure and held across the beat.

Tempo . . . . rate of speed.

Ternary form (ABA) . . a piece divided into three sections: A, B, A.

Tetrachord . . . . a series of four notes having a pattern of whole step, whole step, half step.

Tied notes . . . . notes on the same line or space joined by a curved line and held for the combined values of both notes.

Time signatures . . . . numbers found at the beginning of
($\frac{2}{4}$, $\frac{3}{4}$, $\frac{4}{4}$, $\frac{6}{8}$) a piece or section of a piece. The top number shows the number of beats in each measure. The bottom number shows the kind of note that gets one beat.

Transpose . . . . perform in a key other than the original. Each pitch must be raised or lowered by precisely the same interval, which results in the change of key.

Triad . . . . three-note chord.

Vivace . . . . lively.

Whole step . . . . equal to two half steps; skip one key (black or white).

Appendix D

LIST OF COMPOSITIONS

Index